HARD
SURFACE

HARD
SURFACE
IN SEARCH OF
THE CANADIAN ROAD

PETER UNWIN

KEY PORTER BOOKS

Library and Archives Canada Cataloguing in Publication

Unwin, Peter, 1956–
    Hard surface : in search of the Canadian road / Peter Unwin.

ISBN 978-1-55470-074-5

    1. Roads—Canada—History. 2. Canada—Description and travel.
I. Title.
HE357.U59 2009   388.10971   C2008-906781-9

ONTARIO ARTS COUNCIL
CONSEIL DES ARTS DE L'ONTARIO

THE CANADA COUNCIL | LE CONSEIL DES ARTS
FOR THE ARTS | DU CANADA
SINCE 1957 | DEPUIS 1957

The publisher gratefully acknowledges the support of the Canada Council for the Arts and
the Ontario Arts Council for its publishing program. We acknowledge the support of the
Government of Ontario through the Ontario Media Development Corporation's Ontario
Book Initiative.

We acknowledge the financial support of the Government of Canada through the Book
Publishing Industry Development Program (BPIDP) for our publishing activities.

Every reasonable effort has been made to contact copyright holders. Anyone with infor-
mation on outstanding copyright holders is invited to contact the publisher.
"One For My Baby (And One More For The Road)": lyric by Johnny Mercer; music by
Harold Arlen. © 1943 (Renewed) HARWIN MUSIC CO.
Spanish, Ontario, train station photo: courtesy of Spanish Public Library.
Henry Kelsey stamp © Canada Post Corporation (1993). Reproduced with permission.
Steam buggy stamp © Canada Post Corporation (1970). Reproduced with permission.
Alexander Mackenzie rock carving photo: courtesy of www.johnharveyphoto.com.
"This is not a urinal" ad: courtesy of Washington State Department of Ecology.

Key Porter Books Limited
Six Adelaide Street East, Tenth Floor
Toronto, Ontario
Canada M5C 1H6
www.keyporter.com

Text design: Sonya V. Thursby, Opus House Incorporated
Electronic formatting: Sonya V. Thursby

Printed and bound in Canada
09 10 11 12 5 4 3 2 1

TO EVERY NATURAL FORM, ROCK, FRUIT, OR FLOWER,

EVEN THE LOOSE STONES THAT COVER THE HIGHWAY,

I GAVE A MORAL LIFE.

—WILLIAM WORDSWORTH

A MAN IS, OF ALL SORTS OF BAGGAGE,

THE MOST DIFFICULT TO BE TRANSPORTED.

—ADAM SMITH

THE GETTING OF WISDOM IS A HARD ROAD.

—CLIVE JAMES

CONTENTS

HARD
SURFACE

THERE WILL BE SMOOTH SAILING FOR WE SHALL HAVE
PASSED OVER THE CORDUROY ROADS OF ADVERSITY AND
ONTO THE SMOOTH BITULITHIC PAVEMENTS OF PROSPERITY.
—FORT WILLIAM WEEKLY TIMES JOURNAL, 1898

INTRODUCTION

Since it first wound its way through the Canadian landscape, the road has been represented as a symbol of hope, leading all those who travel on it into a brighter future and a better life. The comforting language of unity and nation building is never far off, and at times a spiritual dimension creeps in. Canadian roads—"Highways of Hope," "Pavements of Prosperity," or "Dream Roads," as they have been called—are routinely associated with growth, nationhood, and the betterment of the individual. It is assumed almost without question that the road will provide us with an escape route from poverty, from the past, and from the class consciousness of old Europe in particular. It will also guarantee national unity, protect us from the enemy, and provide us with a lot of fabulous scenery along the way.

This is a lot to ask of the road, which, in its most basic aspect, remains what it always was: a way of getting somewhere, a long, narrow, diffuse piece of technology, a machine really, a democratizing machine perhaps, and one that facilitates movement by itself remaining still. But the road is very much a body of beliefs, a secular religion that worships freedom and individuality. It pays tribute to the primary human urge to be in motion and allows us to create a story about ourselves, even requires that we do so: the story of who we are, a summation of all the roads we have travelled, of the turnoffs we've missed, of all the songs we have ever sung, and an inventory of all the people we have travelled with—in short, of our lives.

The inclination of the road is inclusive, leading away from the exclusionary etiquettes of the railway or the brittleness of Old World class divisions. Unlike the rail, the road requires no blind obedience to a rigid schedule set by someone else or the purchase of a ticket from a man in a serge suit who's a slave to his timepiece. We don't stand in line to take it. Like an idea or a sudden passion, the road can be embraced on a whim. A man, a woman, their children, and the pet parrot can pile into the wagon or the car, tie the conjugal mattress to the roof, and at any moment undertake a new life. From Newfoundland to Newfoundout, from Fort McMurray to Hope, British Columbia, the road leads somewhere else—somewhere better.

=||=

The early boosters of the Canadian road were governors and military men determined to keep Canada safe from the rabble of American revolutionaries and republicans in the south. A century and a half later, they were followed by ardent enthusiasts of the motor car who understood that without roads, and lots of them, the object of their enthusiasm would remain idle in the barn or putter about on unpaved concession roads, getting hauled out of the mud, with embarrassing frequency, by horses. Many of the early cars came out of the factory with a whip socket built in (but no whip provided), admitting in advance that getting hauled about by a horse was a very likely event.

The more literate and patriotic of road boosters were blatant supporters of the Dominion and the glory of the British Empire. In the road, particularly one that spanned Canada from coast to coast, they saw a chance to put "the granary of the world" to good use by feeding the rest of the Empire. They also saw the road as a sure-fire means to preserve and advance the superiority of what they confidently called their "race."

Today, the belief that building or rebuilding roads will pave the way to a better and more fulfilling life is still with us. It is seen in road construction signs that tell us that all this industrial debris, these scattered tractors, these hard-hatted men who don't seem to be doing anything in particular are in fact *Building a Better Ontario* or *Working Together for a Better Canada,* expressing the basic belief that a better road and a better life are indistinguishable. This belief has been only slightly tempered by time. A 1984 publication of the Ontario Ministry of Transportation tones down its haughtier Empire-building rhetoric and states, shrewdly enough, that the building of roads will at least have a very definite impact on people's "spending habits." The authors were right, just as the highway boosters before them were right, but they were right in ways they could not have predicted. The Highways of Hope have not made Canada the breadbasket of the world, and the Empire has been deconstructed, but the roads are still getting built, widened, or twinned. Today they are bigger, more numerous, more deadly, and more costly to maintain than ever.

$$=\!\!+\!\!=$$

On the side of any one of these roads has waited a girl with a bus ticket in her hand, or even with her thumb out. She has a few dollars in her pocket, and the rest of her life is in front of her. The life that she is after is one that lies further on, always further on. It is a glorious life, and she understands the road to it will be long and packed with adventures in which she will be the central character. To the drivers that pass her, she appears paltry beneath the great sky, forlorn even, framed by looping telephone cables that arc overtop of her. She is as common as the road, but she is proud, and with a thumb pointed skyward, or a knapsack on her back, she marks herself with the universally optimistic gesture of the hitchhiker, the traveller, the person in motion.

On a brilliant summer morning, she has left Moosomin or Indian Head or Carberry or Rainy River, on her way to Calgary in the hope of escaping everyone who misunderstands her. She is too young for nostalgia to have any tug on her. The dirt roads framed by the blazing summer sumacs, the small town with its memorial from the Great War, its church organ, its batten board and wainscotting, have not yet achieved any meaning. They represent only the routines of her life, in which it seems that all poetry has been banished. Without having thought about it, she knows that the poet does not dwell in a fixed abode and that the road is the true dwelling place of the poet, the young, and the vagrant. In Calgary, she eats a makeshift breakfast at a street ministry in a parking lot in Forest Lawn. *Forest Lawn*: in her mind, the two words clang together in opposition. The language of old people, she thinks. The neighbours—old people—are already clamouring to have the ministry shut down. It is too fluid, too much coming and going, too itinerant and youthful. They want things fixed and stationary.

Simply by crossing the highway and facing in the other direction, she changes her destiny. She leaves Thessalon or Chapleau or Shining Tree and rides the Trans-Canada southeast to Toronto, mumbling monosyllabic answers to the questions of well-intentioned drivers as they navigate the thin pastoral strip of highway that follows the North Channel. The pre-twilight sun casts a heartbreaking cover of light on the land and the barn sides. To the south of her is Manitoulin, the Island of the Spirits. Close to shore, the gulls stand knee-deep in the water. She has no idea of the ghosts that inhabit this place, or of the otter that returned from the bottom of the great lake with mud in its jaw and began the world that she is being driven through. The road she travels marks the separation of the deer from the moose, as the man seated next to her attempts to explain, describing how the deer hunters will park on the south side of this highway and moose hunters on the north. She nods. None of it matters to her. None of it surprises her. She is on the road to somewhere else, about to end up sitting on the sidewalk on Yonge Street, the longest main street in the world, named after a man who never set foot in Canada. A tattoo of a rose will soon show on the small of her back, a ring in her nose, and a large dog will be curled up beside her. The road will deposit her here at this blurry intersection between the child and the runaway.

The highway that links this place to her parents' home was built to facilitate her country's passage into a great future. It has done that. It has facilitated the scatterings of sons and daughters. It has left a vague feeling of dissatisfaction and the belief that anything is possible, that a country, like a lover, can be experienced from top to bottom. It has also created its own legacy of death, loneliness, lost children, and indifferent grownups. She is a sample of it—she is literally a "street person," part of the great unaccountable cargo of the road that is not open to inspection and cannot be measured in weigh stations. In all her confusion, she is among the truest, the most common, and perhaps the most meaningful of all the goods the road will deliver. She is part of the social cargo of the Canadian highway—a cargo that is weighted with tears and memory.

By climbing aboard a bus or putting out her thumb, she has joined the great moving community that travels ceaselessly along the road in search of something better, to escape intolerance, or to give vent to their own confusion and even, like the early road promoters insisted, to build a better life. She has put her faith and future in a numbered highway that, in the moment she stands on it, seems to have been built for the sole purpose of accommodating her imperishable youthfulness. It leads to the only place that finally matters—*herself*. She is sixteen years old and has no premonition that this same road may take her back, years from now, wiser and prodigal, humbled by what she has seen and done, carrying her own cargo of stories and experience, as she hurries back to her childhood home, nervous and conflicted.

=‖=

In writing *Hard Surface*, I did not deliberately set out on any record-breaking or newsworthy car rides. I did not consciously set out to either find or lose myself on the road, having already accomplished that several times before this. Nor did I walk, run, rollerblade, skateboard, hitchhike, bicycle, or even unicycle across the country. Instead, I tried to find the Canadian road and figure out what, if anything, it might possibly mean. I skidded left and right for a few hundred miles on the loose gravel of the Trans-Labrador ("Grade *A* gravel," the locals told me repeatedly and proudly). I drove beneath a waterfall that crashed on the hood of my rented car while crossing Vancouver Island. To my shame, I was forced to race wildly down a dirt road north of Lake Superior after impaling my wife in the neck with a fish hook. As I sped to the hospital at Chapleau, I frantically and repeatedly sounded the horn to scatter the bears foraging on the road ahead of me. At the hospital, I learned that fishing mishaps involving hooks are the single most common cause of emergency hospital visits in the North, more common, it would seem, than car accidents. The attending nurse called the doctor at home, where he had just sat down to dinner with his family. "He'll be here in five minutes," she said pleasantly, and five minutes later, there he was. With considerable wit, I explained to the doctor that ordinarily I was a catch-and-release man, but in the case of my wife, I'd decided to keep her. The doctor looked at the fish hook protruding from her neck, and after a moment said sternly, "Maybe you should just go sit down in that chair and not say anything." It was one of those moments where the road had facilitated its old dialogue between town and country. In this case, the Country had trumped the City decisively, and I went and sat in the chair and didn't say anything.

In another escapade, I had the good fortune to drive in a pickup truck from Iqualuit to Annex, Nunavut, where the unmistakable red roofs of the old Hudson's Bay Company trading sheds showed on the desolate shore below. It was a ten-minute ride unless the weather changed, in which case it could become a three-day ordeal that required a helicopter to fly you out.

During a city-wide Toronto blackout, I stood at the corner of Dovercourt and Dupont and watched intense rush-hour traffic pass through the intersection with greater speed, comfort, and efficiency then it ever did when the traffic lights were working.

In other words, I have done what Canadians do: the almost mandatory 15,000-kilometre return trip across Canada, repeated two or three times; the quarter of a million kilometres picked up here and there on camping trips and the way to the store—nothing that remotely compares to the trans-Canadian treks of an average Canadian rock band. Today, aging bass players and drummers recall the days when they transported exotic dancers out of remote taverns in Northern Ontario in exchange for laughter, conversation, and the smell of perfume. The adventure is most often found in the aftermath, in the work the imagination does once the miserable fifteen-hour ride in the rain from Marathon to Kingston is over and we are free to tell ourselves what a remarkable time we had.

In my soundings of the Canadian road, I presumed my real journey was to be by foot, walking the two city blocks to my local library on Roncesvalles Avenue, a predominantly Polish-Canadian street named by an Englishman who fought in the Spanish Peninsular War. Those blocks, house-proud and gorgeous, are mantled by a massive spread of maple trees in precisely the way the street's planner had envisioned when horses, not cars, packed the city roads and shade, not air conditioning, kept the city cool. In Canada, libraries were then called Mechanics' Institutes. The word meant something significantly different then, but as a writer researching a book on the Canadian road, I was pleased by the overlap. To my surprise, I found almost nothing in the libraries: an M.A. thesis, published fifteen years ago, which was a focused and scrupulous account of the economic significance of the building of the Trans-Canada highway; and a single unsatisfying but well-intentioned volume titled *The History of Canadian Roads*, by Edwin C. Guillet, published forty years ago and now long out of print, a book that assumes from the start that roads and human progress are precisely the same thing.

It became clear almost at once that the road had attracted little interest as a phenomenon in itself. About the vehicles that travel the surface of roads, cars in particular, there is no end of information, speculation, and theorizing. One breathless book after another either champions or, more likely, demonizes the car, the culture of the car, and the car-building industry. The road is barely mentioned, and if it is, it is as a banality, an afterthought of no significance in itself, merely a platform from which people can observe the country as it passes and then, more often than not, write another book about it.

In Canada, the road has been further eclipsed by an almost institutionalized love affair with the railway and the iconic Last Spike. This love affair, which is entirely absent in the United States, includes a century of romanticizing oddball characters such as William Cornelius Van Horne, an American who smoked foot-long cigars and, in his mad moments, believed himself to have gone mano-a-mano with Jesse James. In such an environment, even to question the iconic status of the rails feels un-Canadian, as if we are personally slapping Pierre Berton in the face.

There is also the lasting memory of the interminable dullness of too many interminable car rides that can blunt our willingness to see in the road anything more than a surface of grey pavement punctuated by identically dreary and overpriced motels that either do or do not have satellite TV and wireless Internet. This is not to deny that many people have ridden or thumbed the roads of Canada—or at least the Trans-Canada Highway—and that many of them, probably *too* many, have written books about what they saw out the window of the car or the meals they ate or the people met, or any combination of the above. But about the road itself as an idea, what its purpose is, or its meaning, there is nothing at all. As a result, researching and writing about the Canadian road involved many delightful and hair-raising, bumper-to-bumper rides on what used to be called the information superhighway but now, in its ubiquity, is barely called anything at all.

In that massive Babelonian traffic jam, I uncovered information about the aliens who abducted Mike the friendly moose hunter from the Canol Road in northern British Columbia. The aliens who did this were the "typical grey-type aliens," as opposed to the aliens by the edge of the road, who tended to be "more insectoid." While there is plenty of information about the efficacy of the road as a landing platform for flying saucers, there is no clue, for example, as to who was Canada's first casualty of a road collision. And if you are fortunate enough to type in www.umassedu/ --nrec/pdf_files/tws_ strategy_ms_pdf, you could read some very sensible people discussing strategies for the "mitigation of highway impact on wildlife." I began to see that, to some people, the road was something that needed to be "mitigated." I also discovered an interesting photograph of a car that had been hit by a plane and still had the aircraft protruding from it, as well as a quote from an Arctic truck driver who had once seen an upside-down rainbow from the window of his vehicle.

I had considerably less luck uncovering any previous thought or research on the racial aspect of the road, and the role the road plays in community and the destruction of community. There was very little on the psychology of the road, its effects on families or marriage, its relationship to the stranger, or to the soul, or to memory, to the creation and erasing of memory. I found nothing about what happens to us when we travel a road, nothing about escape and oblivion, or the passage of time or what waits in front of us, or what it means to take to the hard surface and leave ourselves behind. Or if that's even possible.

My aim in writing this book was to tape some of those questions to the windshield and go.

（1）

WINDSHIELD TIME

In the summer of 2004, an Alberta poet, Tate Young, was driving a borrowed car between Banff and Edmonton when he was blind-sided by a laundry truck. His last memory of that day is exchanging pleasantries with the ambulance driver and asking him a number of questions about the ambulance he was being rushed to the hospital in. Moments later, he lost consciousness.

Nine days later, he was released from hospital, alive but somehow different. He understood that a new destiny lay in front of him, and that to achieve it he must transform himself into a new man. That person, Mingus Tourette, would be an embodiment of flowing jazz and spontaneous wordplay. Several days after getting out of hospital, he attended an automobile auction and there, in a stroke of good luck, managed to put a successful bid on a fully functional 1986 Chevy C-30 one-ton ambulance. Tate Young, now Mingus Tourette, drove it home, painted it shocking pink, stenciled **write the nation tour** in black letters on the side, fixed a vanity plate to the back that said MINGUS, and set out on a four-week, 15,000-kilometre drive across Canada in the firm belief that Canadian poetry was in a desperate "state of emergency" and that something needed to be done about it at once.

Like most North Americans, Mingus understood that it was crucial to take to the road. He had no doubts about the curative effect of the highway, or that covering—or at least whipping alongside—vast, numbing amounts of land would regenerate him. He was like a character in one of his own poems, stuck

Somewhere in southern suburbia
with a Molotov cocktail in one hand
and a pitchfork in the other

He also knew that the road would whisk him far away from suburbia to that small, crucial town that goes by the name Somewhere Else and lies invitingly just a little bit farther down the highway, past the next gas station, a mile or two after the four-way, a safe distance from the mess we've made of things back home. He knew, as the young always know, that poetry isn't something you write or read or study but something you *do*. It requires brazen stamina, gas in the tank, a blind faith in movement, and the ability to talk breathlessly and all night. Of Mingus, it would require an endless amount of coffee and cigarettes, and at times it would leave him "*naked and drunk / face down on somebody's lawn.*" It would also bring him "*close to the ground and invincible.*"

By the time he set out on his journey, Mingus Tourette had published a book of poetry called *Nunt,* the cover of which shows a young nun wearing high heels and a gas mask, lifting her habit high to display nyloned thighs. "Knee-jerk offensiveness masquerading as a philosophical stance," is how the *Calgary Herald* described it. The *Winnipeg Free Press* was less dismissive, and would have actually reprinted lines from the book were it not for "the sheer volume of profanity and graphic sexual content," which, in the paper's opinion, made it impossible to quote anything.

But Mingus had already passed beyond the censure of the tongue-clucking media. He was transformed. He was now, in his own words, "*a notorious drunkard and effervescent fuckaroo, purveyor of fine apostasy, a thanophobic bastard, and emphatic graphomaniac and chronic neologist.*" He was also behind the wheel of a one-ton pink ambulance barrelling east along the Trans-Canada Highway.

In the big spaces between small towns, the poet took long looks out the window at the double-sloped Prairie barns with their gambrel roofs, designed to accommodate more hay than their single-sloped Eastern counterparts. He whipped through the grand city of Winnipeg, nosing the wide, windy streets beneath the rusticated temple tops of the old commercial buildings and run-down beer

taverns. All the while, he took mental notes of the signs: Chicago Style Blues, Rooms $30 a Night (No guests, No bathroom). Graffitied on the side of a derelict warehouse: Wasted Heritage. Hurtig's Scientific Fur Vault. Winnipeg: Aboriginal—Always and Forever.

He aimed his ambulance through a stalled avenue of remote glass and steel skyscrapers, and then he was out of it and eventually reached Portage La Prairie, where he saw the world's largest Coca-Cola can towering over the Prairies. He saw massive cattle farms and old grain elevators, standing upright like secular churches. Then he was tumbling into mixed, gnarly bush, dimpled with dunes, eclipsed by a massive junkyard of scrapped cars. On the north side of the highway, eight black colts danced on the prairie. A few more cropped the grass indifferently, their tails wagging as if they were laughing at something—him, perhaps. Then a cloud of rooks, suspended in mid-air, expanded and shrank like a jellyfish.

Soon Mingus found that he was reading every sign that he passed. At times he was depressed by the sheer numbing conformity of the commercial language that had been knitted over his country—the language was all dead language and appeared on billboards that were dead too, obscuring the land, *his* land, blocking out his birthright. *We put the* WIN *in Winnipeg.* Yes, he thought. Maybe you did. But who put the dirt in the dirty water?

Who wrote this language, he wondered, and why were they not taken out and forced to perform community service for their crimes? Everywhere he looked, the same towering signs promoted the same automobiles, the same lube jobs, the same fried chicken and muffler repairs. The same McMonstrous fast-food joints had metastasized from Toronto to Sicamous, British Columbia; desperate "Family Restaurants" with their obligatory "Home cooking."

(What the hell did they do? Cook it at home and then drive it to the restaurant?)

Mingus was becoming cranky with all the obligatory alliteration and the feel-good, can't-lose propositions streaming past the windshield—Chicken Charlie's ("at Chicken Charlie's it's always happy hour!")—but he was also starving and forced himself to stop, only to discover that Chicken Charlie's wasn't so much happy as it was miserable. The chicken was miserable, the obligatory coleslaw was miserable, the waitress was miserable, the little throwaway vinegar and ketchup sacks, the little plastic buckets to sit in were all miserable. The coffee was more than miserable. Everyone in the place was miserable, the tin music coming from the tinny speakers was miserable, and it was all made more miserable by the signs that insisted how wonderful it was. The cruellest desecration of all—Mingus had always suspected this—is the desecration of language. Why not just spit it out: At Miserable Charlie's, we serve Miserable Chicken. Sorry. Why not, he wondered, tell the truth: Life is very short and then you die, usually after a prolonged and debilitating illness. What was so hard about telling the truth? If poets could do it, how hard could it really be?

Eventually, the language of the road became more diverse and Mingus was cheered by a billboard that shot by at 120 kilometres an hour: Raid Kills Bugs Dead. He grinned, remembering the old Lew Welch short story by the same name. From Welch, he was off into the undying legacy of the Beats, of Neal Cassady and his teenage wife, LuAnne, of Gary Snyder, who roomed with Lew Welch, of Ginsberg, of Kerouac, of the stunning Vicki Russell, who after getting arrested was described in the New York papers as "a six-foot marijuana-smoking redhead." *On the Road*, off the road, they were road freaks, every one of them. The Beats, and the beat beat beat of miles as they knocked beneath the ambulance made Mingus smile again. He was thinking of Lew Welch's jeep, the one he called "Willie," of the suicide note he had placed in his vehicle, containing the enigmatic clue "I went Southwest. Goodbye." He thought of the shotgun, the body that was never found. (How is it possible, he wondered, to shoot yourself and not have your body found? Perhaps it was a skill required of every poet.) From there he pondered the dead union leaders and Mafiosi whose bodies were reportedly chipped into the smooth tarmac flowing beneath him.

He was thinking about the allure of the road and considering his Canadian colleagues and predecessors, from the early hitch-hikes of Stompin' Tom Connors, back in the day when the local police would take him off the side of the road, put him up for a night in jail, and in the morning provide him with a chit for coffee and breakfast at a local restaurant. He thought of Al Purdy and all the Cariboo Horses they'd ride; of ct staples, the inventor of the can-opener alarm clock and composer of the fragmented beat verse "Cathartic Reflections in a 3 a.m. Greyhound Window (somewhere between Kamloops and Jasper)," a poet who knew

the delirious overdose
of being thrown thru
a car window
in the mountains of idaho

The verse reminded Mingus of a story he had heard out of Espanola, Ontario, where Highway 6 comes to an end, intersecting the Trans-Canada at a gruesome Tim Hortons. The story concerned a rugged, hard-drinking woman who had been ejected through the front windshield of her car—twice, in two separate accidents. He remembered that ct staples had once tried to travel north hobo-style but had hopped the wrong train and ended up in the U.S. Southwest, where he had himself cleansed in a Navajo sage ceremony. Only on the highway, thought Mingus, can you have any faith that you are not lost. He tried to imagine the many thousands of miles they had all logged, the turns, and the wrong turns. A line from F.R. Scott's poem "Trans Canada" floated up from his memory:

I have sat by night beside a cold lake
and touched things smoother than moonlight on still water

He wondered, as did F.R. Scott a half century before him, whether all roads led to the sun.

As he travelled across the shining country, Mingus's pink ambulance became a trans-Canada versificationmobile, picking up poets, runaways, and self-described "independent literary editors," all of them in a hurry, all of them disciples of the road. With Mingus at the wheel, they engaged in the quintessential intimacy of two people in the front seat of a moving vehicle. The time meshed perfectly with the kilometres that tapped metronome-like in beat with their conversations.

Four billion years worth of granite whipped alongside them. The passenger inserted a tape or a CD or twiddled the radio dials for reception, or snapped the lids off takeout coffees. The talk between the two of them became modulated to the passing landscape. The blue, the black, and infinite shades of green washed over them and allowed for interludes of silence, fragments of talk that started and then stopped, like roads that led nowhere but were still enjoyable for the simple fact of their existence, and for the likelihood that all of them went somewhere you would never go. Mingus's mother had a term for these long, leisurely drives where two people engage in the intimate and unhurried talk that the passage of miles elicits. "Windshield time," she called it. There was nothing she liked better than to share some "quality windshield time" with an old friend.

Beside him, the passenger had his knees up, his feet on the dash or out the window. He was struck by the thought that when you are travelling the highway, you never grow old. Only in constant motion does time ever come to a stop. If he was to stay on the road, he would remain thirty-six forever.

For four weeks, the poet delivered himself and his passengers to readings. He attempted mad and inspirational distances, including an almost hallucinatory dash that saw him read in Montreal on a Friday night and again in Brandon, Manitoba, less than forty-eight hours later. His pink ambulance stopped at places called The Dreg's Café, Modern Fuel, and the Ghetto Lounge, where poets spilled out and read from books, their own books, titled *Runaway, Velocity, Any Place Beyond Ourselves,* and *Wonder Walker*, names that honoured the necessity of movement, the essential glamour of seeing ourselves in motion, and the primacy of the road as the only—or at least the cheapest and most accessible—conduit to freedom. The pace was as gruelling as that of the voyageurs on their fur-seeking sweeps from Montreal to the Lakehead, disappearing into the fog at Port au Chapeau with their paddles hitting the water at sixty-five strokes a minute, eighteen hours a day, all portages taken on the run, stepping ruthlessly over their fallen comrades. Just like writers, thought Mingus.

Winnipeg one night, Thunder Bay the next. From Thunder Bay down the spectacular North Shore to St. Catharines, with Garnet Rogers on the CD player, "Night Rides" playing over and over again, a tribute to Rogers's brother, who had died so terribly on the tarmac of a Cincinnati airport. Mingus noticed once more how the hallucinatory repetition of the guitar duplicated the passing of every telephone pole, turning the song into the very road itself with its numbing repetition and impossible dreams of motion, the shadows that chunk across the windshield and then are gone. Toronto again, back and forth on Queen Street, sharing the road with trucks and bicycles, in-line skaters, streetcars, skateboarders, electric wheelchairs, an unelectric wheelchair pulled by an eager pair of silver-blue husky dogs, policemen mounted on horses, children in wagons, their immense eyes shining like satellite dishes, taking in the teeming road, transmitting it.

Mingus's pink ambulance was at once engulfed in the poetry of city streets: the stunning, bare-shouldered girls with MP3 players attached to their biceps, sure-footed on rollerblades, angling right and left, their hips and hair swaying in opposite directions. They looked as elegant as schooners tacking into the pure black tarmac of the city. Mingus smiled. He would write his own *On the Road*; he would call it A Saga of Cities, Streets, and the Bebop Night.

Mingus sat at the wheel with a microphone in his hand, broadcasting his message to the streets of Toronto: "Poetry, poetry, free poetry coming at you. Tonight, the Gladstone Hotel, free poetry, poetry." The Toronto police grinned at him, and to Mingus this demonstrated an agreeable height of urban and even Eastern sophistication—it is illegal for a non-emergency vehicle to be equipped with a red light and a working public address system. But the road, he thought, like speech itself, had to be free. "Free poetry," he boomed, "coming at ya, coming at ya."

Like the priests who had accompanied the fur traders, Mingus and his fellow poets crossed the highways of Canada to spread the word of a mysterious God. It was a fight for the souls of the people—it always had been, leading them away from the heathen gods of the mind-numbing mini-mart and the apostasy of the television and newspapers. Mingus knew, as did the old Oblats, who sent their missionaries by dogsled into a roadless land, that "Souls cost dear, and they have to be purchased one by one."

Fifteen thousand kilometres later, Mingus Tourette was back in Edmonton, where he was immediately pulled over by a city police officer. "I assume you're in a rock 'n' roll band or something," said the officer, stern-faced, humourless, and wearing his obligatory wraparound, road-black shades. Mingus related the story of his epic journey to save Canadian poetry from the clutches of schoolteachers, part-time professors and untouchable literary superstars and concluded it strategically with that bright afternoon in Toronto where he blared his P.A. and flashed his lights while the local police grinned at him. "It was on the news," said Mingus. "CTV, CBC Radio, and everything!"

"And nobody called you on it?" demanded the officer, flaunting his contempt for his Toronto colleagues as he wrote Mingus a $178 ticket for displaying an emergency red light on a non-emergency vehicle.

"No," said Mingus, "you're the first. Congratulations."

NOW READER READ FOR I AM WELL ASSUR'D
THOU DOST NOT KNOW THE HARDSHIPS I ENDUR'D.
—HENRY KELSEY, 1693

FEET ON THE GROUND:
THE ROADLESS ROAD

On the twelfth of June in 1690, a twenty-three-year-old man left York Fort, on the west coast of James Bay, and undertook the most commonplace of human activities: he put himself in motion. Like most travellers, he set out to see things. In this regard, he would be spectacularly successful. Aside from the dwarfing expanse of the boreal plains, the last outcroppings of the Canadian Shield, the sheer, treeless contours of the Arctic, and the grasslands of the Canadian Prairies, he would become the first European to see a grizzly bear. ("An outgrown Bear," he noted, "he is mans food & he makes food of man.") He was the first Englishman to see Saskatchewan, the first to see a bison, the first to see a buffalo hunt, and the first to leave a written record of a muskox. It is speculated that during this journey, which took two years, he travelled a path that roughly follows Highway 9 in northern Saskatchewan (the route is today dotted with Doukhobor cemeteries), turned around some twelve miles south of what is now The Pas, Manitoba, and walked and paddled back, a distance of some 1,200 miles (or nearly 2,000 kilometres).

In making this astonishing journey, Henry Kelsey, a young Hudson's Bay Company fur trader, ensured himself a place in history. He also established himself as one of the first and certainly one of the most successful Canadian tourists. Evelyn Waugh's dictum that the "tourist is always the other fellow" in this case did not apply. There *was* no other fellow—at least, not one who was writing down his daily observations in a notebook.

By the 1680s, Kelsey was already familiar to his superiors as a man extremely sympathetic with, even smitten by, Natives—their customs, languages, and way of life. To the all-powerful London Committee of the Hudson's Bay Company, overseeing operations from England, he was known as "a very active lad, Delighting much in Indian compa., being never better pleased than when hee is Travelling amongst them." It was also known that he had a fondness for walking immense distances, his credentials as an inveterate walker having been established in the late 1680s, when he and a Native companion, a boy, undertook a winter journey to carry a packet east from York Fort to New Severn on the coast of Hudson Bay. Prior to Kelsey, three Natives had attempted this trip, and all had failed. In 1689, Kelsey and the same boy disembarked from the *Hopewell* somewhere north of the Churchill River and began to walk north, hugging the shore of the bay in the hope of bringing "to a Commerce ye Northern Indians . . . and also ye dogside Nation." The two covered, in Kelsey's estimation, 138 miles north and 142 on the return, followed by 93 more to the Churchill River. The trip took a month.

Kelsey's journey was also accomplished without the benefit of a road, or even a need for one. The human foot is a versatile technology, even more so if it is shod in the moccasins that in winter Kelsey himself would hand out to his men. In tough times, they could always be eaten. Kelsey was discovering what the Natives he so admired had long demonstrated: that the earth is a vast road, but it runs slower than the rivers. These rivers, the Ottawa, the St. Lawrence, the Madawaska, and many others, were the first major commercial roads of Canada, the celebrated "mast highways" on which the great red and white pines of Canada would travel on a lengthy journey that would see them transformed into the masts of British ships and the doorframes and windowsills of Europe.

By taking these combined roads of earth and water, Kelsey seemed to be consoling something fundamental in himself: the human urge to be in motion, to move, to see, to acquire an understanding or at least a glimpse of what neither he nor any other European had seen before. To his superiors, however, his mission was nothing so lyrical. He was ordered to "search diligently for Mines, Minerals or Drugs of what Kind soever, and to bring Samples of them down with him." In return, he was to pack, among other things, a pair of handcuffs, thirty pounds of Brazilian tobacco, two pairs of "sissers," and three ivory combs. He was, in short, on a trade mission.

He was also instructed to make contact with an unknown Siouan tribe, the Nawatayme Poets, to help them make peace with their enemies and to bring them "to a Commerce." The name is perhaps a phonetic simplification of a longer and more complex Siouan word. It is also a reminder that one of the first and greatest Canadian traverses, like the barrelling and raucous tour of Mingus Tourette, was more than peripherally connected to poetry. In Kelsey's time, the term *poets* was sometimes affixed to the names of Native tribes.

Further, the young Kelsey, in a bizarre move that has never been entirely explained, did something no explorer before or since has ever done: he wrote the prologue to his daily journal in rhyming couplets of decasyllabic tetrameter.

> *In sixteen hundred & ninety'th year*
> *I set forth as plainly may appear*
> *Through God's assistance for to understand*
> *The natives language & to see their land*

In attempting this journal, Kelsey had stumbled into a new literary pathway, since his notes were taken a century and a half before a written tradition of the explorer's report had begun to develop. He was, in a sense, free to write in any manner he wanted:

> *For many times I have often been opprest*
> *With fears & Cares yt I could not take my rest*
> *Because I was alone & no friend could find*
> *And once yt in my travels I was left behind*
> *Which stuck fear & terror into me.*

Later, when his ninety-line rhyming prologue comes to an end, Kelsey reverts to a type of abbreviated English prose in which he describes at one point *"one Indian lying a dying."* The unfortunate man endures his suffering for two days before death takes him. The young, ill-educated Kelsey strikes a remarkably moving funeral cadence when he writes quietly, *"Last night death ceased & this morning his body was burned according to their way."*

It is obvious to scholars now that Kelsey could not have made his remarkable inland trek had he not been in the company of Natives. In fact, Kelsey's great journey was part of a vast annual migration by Plains First Nations from the interior to the bay, a journey that today very few people would dream of making, by air, rail, or road, if there were a road, let alone by foot. He was in the company of a people whose own feet had not yet been separated from the earth by a macadamized sheath. Every pebble was felt, every twig made its impression on the foot, and every step was fraught with danger. Even the Iroquois Book of Rites, which predates Columbus's arrival in the New World by half a century, acknowledges the difficulty of contemporary locomotion by congratulating all those travellers who have managed to negotiate the forest and who have survived "wild beasts ... thorny ways and falling trees." The vast highway of the earth itself was as readable to them as the road signs that so fussily and so thickly block the view on today's Trans-Canada: upon finding a footprint, Kelsey's companions confidently state that it was put there "four Days past."

Kelsey's celebrated journey through the remote Barren Lands—a name he seems to have coined—was made possible by a highly mobile and interconnected grouping of various tribes, upon whom he was entirely dependent. The group in which he travelled encountered many neighbouring tribes who already knew of Kelsey's journey, indicating an efficient system of message sending, a runner perhaps, whose smooth passage over a roadless surface had a centuries-long history. When Cortez touched shore in 1519, runners had within twenty-four hours provided descriptions of his ships, men, and weapons to Montezuma, 300 miles (nearly 500 kilometres) away. Iroquois runners carried news from the Atlantic seaboard to the Niagara frontier, loping day and night through the dense mantle of the forest, looking up long enough to navigate by the stars.

The human urge to cover land is uniquely manifested in the many great Native distance runners, from Tom Longboat to Jim Thorpe to Louis Tewanima, who, at the age of eighty, is said to have walked twenty miles a day herding sheep and routinely run 120 miles barefoot, just to watch the trains pass. At the age of ninety he died, fittingly enough, by falling off a mountain. Running vast distances, like walking itself, carries with it a mythical and even mystical dimension that links the traveller with the universe in ways that are not always comprehensible. In the last century, there were reports of a Native runner from southern California who left Cottonwood Island in Nevada at sunrise, only to arrive at Fort Yuma at the exact same moment that he left.

To cover land by foot in particular is to engage in a type of physical mystery. Walking itself is a more prosaic form of dance. This was convincingly demonstrated in the summer of 1870 when a Métis scout was sent out from Fort Garry to Headingly, approximately twenty kilometres away. He was armed with a surveyor's pedometer to determine with greater accuracy the distance between the two settlements. On his return the next morning from Headingly, folks at Fort Garry were astonished to discover that the pedometer clocked in not at forty kilometres but at a lofty 185. When questioned, the Métis guide explained simply, "I went to a dance." In a single evening, on a scuffed wooden floor, with fiddles groaning, he had covered 145 kilometres.

The greatest, or certainly one of the most astonishing, walkers the world has ever known was the peripatetic Englishman John "Walker" Stewart, who, aside from possessing the reputed ability to be in more than one place at the same time, also walked around the earth, perhaps more than once, even making a brief traverse through the wilds of Canada. Ostensibly he walked the planet for the purpose of burying the books he had written. Stewart, who makes a brief appearance in Wordworth's book-length poem *The Prelude*, was also pals with both Coleridge and de Quincey. De Quincey even offered to translate Stewart's writings into Latin so his ideas would be comprehensible for all of eternity. These books, to be buried six feet deep to protect them from the state, contained Stewart's theories on the transmutability of the human personality, which he considered a complete illusion. Stewart, who was found dead in a London hotel room surrounded by the paraphernalia of opium addiction, stands as somewhat disconcerting proof of the connection between transformation and travel.

Austrian author René Freund walked 1,138 kilometres to reach Santiago de Compostela in Spain, on a road that was once thought literally to reach the end of the world. Freund observed that "walking is the form of travel most suited in pace to perception ... You measure the world step by step."

Except for the occasional raft or canoe ride, this is what Kelsey did, step by step, day after day, month after month. Often, he and his companions were lost, mystified by a thick matrix of trails left by buffalo, who had established their own roads on the land long before Kelsey. It is likely that in making his way across Manitoba and half of Saskatchewan, he gave way to that warm personal bond that develops among travellers, foot travellers in particular— a bond that is evoked by Chaucer in *The Canterbury Tales*—a sense that all motion is a type of pilgrimage. It is tempting to imagine how this bond manifested itself during Kelsey's trek, how windshield time was achieved between himself and his fellow travellers, the songs perhaps, the sharing of stories, the smoking, the witticisms, the interplay of language. Kelsey, the first European to observe and write about the customs of the Plains peoples, and the very first of many Hudson's Bay Company employees to record his observations of First Nations religion and life, seems to have spent his time forever grilling his companions on such diverse subjects as the nature of heaven, the allotments of different meats to men and women, and what happens to a woman after she dies, as compared to a man. Perhaps even the romance of the road did not escape him, for somehow, in the loneliness of vast land, it seems that all travel is a search for love. In his later journals, Kelsey would admit guiltily to his rather miserable loneliness in regard to a certain Native woman who was absent on her own journey.

Young Henry Kelsey and his colleagues managed to make the decent pace of six to thirty miles (ten to nearly fifty kilometres) a day, and twenty-five a day on the plains, measuring his distance in miles and *pikes*, a vanished term of measurement that lives on in *turnpike* and the old slang expression *to pike along*, meaning "to hurry." The North American continent was his highway, the tribes of the New World were his constant road companions, guiding and influencing every step that he made, removing from his very feet his clunky British boots and replacing them with moccasins. For nearly the next two centuries, any traverse across Canadian soil or water would be accomplished in this manner, with the guidance of Cree, Mohawk, Ojibway, and members of other First Nations. Not until the newcomers got their own feet more firmly planted on the ground were they able to minimize the help they received from Canadian Natives. More than a century and a half later, Paul Kane was approached on his enormous cross-Canada painting trek by an Ojibway medicine man who offered to provide him six days of favourable wind in exchange for a single plug of tobacco. Kane, an irrepressible traveller himself, made the deal with the medicine man and commenced his journey under the promised favourable wind. But Kane was very much a white man, very much the modern Canadian traveller. Unlike Kelsey, he did not set himself upon the land to be changed by the people who lived in it. He was possessed of full confidence in the conventions of 19th-century society and the confines of his own European paintbox. For Paul Kane, to be given a good wind in exchange for tobacco was a barely amusing coincidence.

Kelsey was of a different ilk. Unlike so many who came after him, his journey was not undertaken to demonstrate his own superiority to what he encountered. His direction, from the start, tended to be headfirst into the unknown. He was, wrote historian Gerald Morton, "Our first example of that comparatively rare species, the Indianized Englishman." It is easy to forget that the interactions of these different cultures, which, we are told, have crushed out the Native worldview, could have equally profound consequences in the other direction. On his great overland journey, which placed him firmly in the book of history, Kelsey achieved the aim of every traveller: to know more than himself, to encounter dimensions in life that had been previously unknown and inscrutable. "Every [Indian] man," he wrote after carefully listening to his Native companions, "Maketh his own songs by Vertue of what he dreams."

This coolly observed statement constitutes one of the first written attempts in the English language to describe the ways of the indigenous people of North America. And it is achieved exclusively through travel, with a tourist's eye open wide, not in search of comfort, but for what is different and memorable, the squirrel dinner, the roasted pigeons, the meal of swans, the sight of eighty tents pitched together on the prairie.

Henry Kelsey died in 1724 at the age of fifty-six in his own home on Church Street in East Greenwich, England, leaving behind a widow and three children. Within a decade, his widow found it necessary to petition the Hudson's Bay Company for financial assistance to help with the cost of apprenticing her son. In his lifelong service to the company, Kelsey had crossed the Atlantic Ocean twelve times and amassed several thousand miles on land, but very little money. In making his memorable trek cross

Canada, he received a gratuity of thirty pounds, making his journey, in the words of one historian, "if not the greatest ... surely one of the cheapest."

BREAKING THE TRAIL:
"ADEQUATE FOR HORSEMEN, BUT
UNSUITABLE FOR WOMEN"

The word *road* derives from the old English *rad*, meaning "ride." Its verb form, *ridan*, gives us "to ride," and between them a close linguistic similarity has coursed across at least five centuries. Today, the roads we have ridden sound to the ear comfortably familiar to the *rads* that were *ridan* by the highwaymen of old or, before them, the whale roads (*hron-r de*) and swan roads (rivers) that Beowulf travelled in his quest to defeat Grendel. *Highway* refers to the medieval main roads of Great Britain, which were built up higher than the earth around them, making them "high ways." Highways were unique in that they were under the protection of the king and open to even the most lowly of travellers. To "take to the highway" did not mean a foray into freedom and personal discovery—

it meant a job with a carriage line. Nor were they interchangeable with *byways*, private roads available for use by a selected few.

=⊨

It was not a highway, a byway, or even a footpath that Sir George Prevost had recourse to in the fall of 1812 when he ordered the 104th Regiment of Foot to begin their drills in preparation for an overland march from Fredericton, New Brunswick, to Quebec City, a distance of nearly a thousand miles (1,600 kilometres) and an "effort," it was called at the time, "yet unknown in British warfare." The drills for this march were undertaken in snowshoes.

Like the moccasin, which the officers of the regiment had already taken to wearing, the snowshoe was another Native technology that concerned itself with the interaction of the human foot and the earth beneath it. Like the moccasin, in desperate times it too could be boiled and eaten. The snowshoe amounted to the equivalent of carrying a winter highway attached to the bottom of your feet, and newcomers to North America were easily convinced of the need for it.

In late February 1813, the bugles of the 104th blew a lament to "The Girls We Leave Behind Us" and the regiment began to march in the deepest snow that had fallen in a decade. It marched, according to eighteen-year-old Lieutenant John Le Couteur, in "Indian file"—a single column, one man behind the other—an expression that has lived for centuries in the North American idiom, suggesting stealth in a dense forest and the absence of roads, or even a footpath wide enough to contain two people abreast. The term implies a certain knowingness, even a *belonging*

in the woods, a superior tactical understanding of how human beings move through the forest. Each squad was also fitted with an
Algonquin *odabaggan*, from which has evolved the French word
tabagan and the barely more Anglicized *toboggan*. As it marched,
the troop extended nearly a half a mile in length.

The first week proved easy going through settled land; there
were even a few scattered barns to sleep in at night. But soon the
snow and the physical reality of marching so many men and supplies through the woods began to take their toll. A soldier toppling
over in his snowshoes could, like a stalled car on a single-lane road,
hold up the line for a quarter of an hour until he regained his upright position. Each man and officer was required to move to the
head of the line for ten or fifteen minutes to break trail. Once this
sweat-producing stint of labour was finished, he stepped one pace
to the side, let the entire company pass, then fell in on a solidly
packed trail with his snowshoes hung over his shoulder. In this regard, the regiment was one continuous road-producing machine
a quarter of a mile in length, foreshadowing a later military operation in the 1940s: the American effort to construct the Alaska
Highway. When asked by skeptical Canadian reporters how he
planned to build a road through the muskeg of British Columbia,
the colonel in charge replied simply, "With six machines of one
thousand men each."

Like so many North American roads, the path that the 104th
beat into the snow closely followed the edge of the rivers and in
some cases was located directly on top of them. In the hope of
profiting from these frozen roads, some innkeepers constructed
temporary "inns" on the ice. Makeshift, clapboard, and prone to
bursting into flames, these establishments were reluctantly aban-

doned by their owners even under the most dire of circumstances. Such owners, insisted settler John Mactaggert, were willing to be swept into oblivion when the ice melted beneath them, "So long as they are catching a farthing," an early observation of the road-side as a premium retail space.

At night, the men of the 104th "hutted," using their snow-shoes as shovels, digging away four or five feet of snow until the ground was reached and piling up the discarded snow as a shel-ter from the wind. On an afternoon in early March, Le Couteur turned an angle of the river and saw that the head of the com-pany had come to a complete standstill. Hastening along, he saw that every soldier in line was seriously frostbitten, including one fellow who was "altogether one ulcerated mass, as if scalded all over from boiling water."

Twenty-four days after setting out from Fredericton, the 104th reached their destination. Quebec, which had not seen its first horse until 1645, had long been accustomed to foot travel as the prevailing mode of transportation. Presumably the overland ar-rival of the 104th came as no great surprise, and was even wel-comed by those few staunch individuals who saw the corrosive effects of progress taking place all around them. By the late 1600s, there had been nearly 200 horses trotting and plowing their way around Quebec—so many, in fact, that the reigning governor ex-pressed concern that the young men of Quebec were losing the ability, and even the art, of walking, either with or without snow-shoes. Had the governor still been alive, he would have been re-lieved by the arrival of the 104th, who were given ten days rest, then ordered to march 200 more miles to a village near Montreal. Having reached that, they were then sent packing for 200 more miles to Kingston. "We are like the children of Israel," commented one exhausted soldier, "we must march forty years before we halt." In fact, the nearly thousand-mile march was accomplished in the remarkable time of six weeks.

In traversing this route, the quick-penned lieutenant was not only heading west to war and the great inland ocean of Lake Ontario (where he was astounded to see the British fleet floating on fresh water), he was also heading directly into his own life.

As might be expected of a curious eighteen-year-old, Le Couteur brought with him to the New World not only a profound interest in things Native, but a very keen eye for the ladies. "The Governor's wife," he generously noted in his diary, "might be about six and thirty, but her looks gave her only thirty." For some reason, the insatiable and endless search for female beauty has been overlooked as a motivating force behind a great deal of Canadian travel, trade, exploration, and even nation building. Presumably those indefatigably lusty voyageurs who put themselves through thirty-five back-breaking portages between Montreal and Grand Portage, often on the run, did so for more than the sake of some greasy bannock or the starvation wages their bosses were paying them.

While the relationship between road building and war has been long considered a given, the softer and more intriguing one between love and motion has not. Le Couteur's journals sing with appreciation of various "splendid girls," in particular the sixteen-year-old Sophie, who, along with her father, was crossing a lake one morning in a rowboat when they were attacked by a bear. What impressed Le Couteur was the remarkable "discretion and courage," with which the sixteen-year-old rammed the point of a boat hook into the bear's eye. Presumably such skills had disappeared from the repertoire of European teenage girls, and Le Couteur's admiration is palpable and keen.

Vast empty distances, loneliness, and the stark absence of women all had their role to play in the hearts of the men who either travelled or constructed the original roads. A straightforward expression of this loneliness was mounted on a fingerboard sign nailed to a fir tree by an American serviceman in the 35th Engineers during the building of the Alaska Highway. The sign, posted above a vast and youthful army of 20,000 men, read

Help Wanted: Female

After falling in love with nearly every woman in Lower and Upper Canada, Lieutenant Le Couteur went on to have a distinguished career in the War of 1812. He also found time to transport an abandoned kitten in a specially made travelling box all the way from Queenston to Fredericton to ease the loneliness of a woman who had recently lost her own cat. This transport, like the meanderings of Le Couteur himself, proves the Canadian road, even from its beginning, was much more than a conduit for the waging of war or the transportation of goods. It was a tangible passageway by which loneliness could be eased and human contact facilitated, a hard-fought route through the forest that, in its highest manifestation, could retrace the deep routes of a passionate heart.

══╪══

The first roads to be built in maritime Canada were crude trails hacked from the dense bush for the simple and even exemplary purpose of delivering mail. This means that some of the first cargo of the Canadian road included, along with the expected cannon and gunpowder, billets-doux, letters home, missives written in the face of loneliness. The mailman appears as one of the first travellers on the road, pushing his lonely way through the deer paths, the tote roads, and finally the road itself, specifically built to accommodate him. In the seventeenth century, one Nova Scotia mailman covered a seventy-two-mile (115 kilometre) route for three months without meeting another human being.

While this raises the question of who exactly the mail was being delivered *to*, the original Canadian road is here presented in its first and long-lasting spiritual aspect: a conduit for verse, for the gossip that makes communication worthwhile in the first place, and for dark letters that announce the death of a loved one. The story also reveals the original Canadian mailman as a mute pioneer troubadour lugging a canvas bag through an almost primordial forest, whistling to remind himself that he's there and to warn the bears of his presence. Joseph Howe describes an old postie named Stewart who worked the route from Pictou to Halifax and carried the mail in his jacket pocket, along with a gun to shoot any partridge that he might encounter. The partridge he sold to his customers as he went along.

In 1606, Champlain and his men built the first graded road in Canada, a ten-mile military route connecting Port Royal to Digby Cape, Nova Scotia. Another century and a half would pass before another road was constructed in Nova Scotia.

Champlain also built a road for the purpose of gaining access to a good fishing hole. It has been postulated, probably incorrectly, that this road, some 2,000 paces long, was the first and last Canadian road constructed for the exclusive purpose of fishing. In reality, the relationship between the road and fishing is complex in Canada. Highway boosters and provincial authorities routinely identified fishing as one of the leading benefits and justifications of a good road system. For some Canadians, a road isn't a road at all if it doesn't lead to a good fishing hole. Champlain, a man of many interests, might have, if given his way, constructed a road designed exclusively for the purpose of birdwatching, such as the road that today runs through Point Pelee National Park on the southernmost tip of Ontario. Champlain, in the absence of such a road, once got himself hopelessly lost in the woods while following the flight of a bird he had never seen before.

On the west coast of North America, the original roads were known as "grease trails." These trails stretched from the Fraser River to Alaska, were well maintained by ancient road crews, and were even identified by individual names. Predating the arrival of Europeans by 4,000 years, the grease that the trails are named after comes from the eulachon, or oolichan (sometimes translated as "salvation fish"), a smelt, also known as "candlefish" for the sheer greasiness of it. Ignite a wick placed in the mouth of a candlefish, and supposedly it will burn through to the tail.

This grease, rendered into an edible fat, was packed into carved cedar containers that resembled tea chests and traded extensively among First Nations throughout the coastal interior in exchange for soapstone, copper, obsidian, and nephrite. Commercial oolichan fisheries still exist today.

It was one of the grease trails that allowed Alexander Mackenzie to reach the Bella Coola River and become the first European on record to cross the North American continent, a feat he accomplished in 1793, twelve years before Lewis and Clark.  Mackenzie knew the value of what he called "a good road," having had to cut at least one of them out of the woods to keep going. A good road, in Mackenzie's estimation, was a beaten path along which "two men could carry a birch bark canoe four miles without resting." The grease trail that Mackenzie and his party took involved a 220-mile (350 kilometre) walk across the inland plateau of British Columbia and resulted in a famous piece of graffiti inscribed on a rock in what is now the Dean Channel of the Pacific Coast.

Mackenzie completed this, the second of his famous Canadian explorations, at the age of twenty-nine. He had travelled by canoe and by foot an estimated 2,300 miles. At the age of forty-eight, he married a fourteen-year-old girl and died seven years later at a roadside inn near Dunkeld, Scotland.

=╪=

Outside of landing the big one, packing out rendered edible fat, and delivering the written word, another of the major physical and psychological reasons for constructing roads in Canada was to rid the landscape of trees. In this tree-affirmative age, we forget that for a great deal of our history the tree has been considered a less-than-friendly neighbour. Christ, after all, was crucified on a cross made from a tree—according to legend, a trembling aspen.

The very reason the aspen trembles, observed Thomas de Quincey, is because it *knows* that Christ was murdered on its back. As the author of "The English Mail-Coach, or, The Glory of Motion," de Quincey knew more than a little about the English road and begins his famous essay by praising a certain Mr. Palmer for accomplishing "two things, very hard to do on our little planet; . . . he had invented mail-coaches, and he had married the daughter of a duke." He also postulates the mail coach as a "national organ for publishing," in that news of mighty events first worked their way into town via these coaches, in the mail, and in the verbal hailings of the coachman himself.

Anna Jameson famously and rather snootily states in her travelogue of an 1836 sojourn, "A Canadian Settler hates a tree, regards it as his natural enemy, as something to be destroyed, eradicated, annihilated by all and any means." She neglects to mention that trees were a leading cause of death in Canada during her time. For centuries, until the automobile accident replaced it, the hatchet wound was Canada's most common source of injury. In 1822, the Military Settling Department had determined that getting "killed by a tree" was a major reason for Canadian depopulation, along with "drowned, deceased," and "gone to the United States." Getting rid of trees was viewed as morally virtuous in itself. In 1763, an east coast traveller was stricken with shame, on the road to Annapolis, to see that it was, in his words, "*embarrassed* with young elders." The road, he reported several years later, "was adequate for horsemen but unsuitable for women."

The egregious quality of early Canadian roads is perhaps unparalleled in history, giving rise to a sort of literary subgenre of insult and invective. It would seem that early Canadians were the worst road builders of all time. "I lately had the misfortune to ride on the roads of this district," complained an 1801 *Niagara Herald* article. To Anna Jameson, a Canadian road was one uninterrupted "black bottomless Slough of despond." "A terrible bog of liquid mud," opined Mrs. Simcoe. "A hell for horses," noted one 1803 visitor to New Brunswick. "Oleaginious pools," noted another. Roads would be routinely cut and then vanish within a generation. To Charles Dickens, the Canadian road was no less fetid than a London slum: "The swamp . . . the perpetual chorus of frogs, the rank, unseemly growth, the unwholesome steaming earth. Here and there, and frequently too, we encountered a solitary broken down wagon." In a charming piece of understatement, Jean Baudoin, a priest involved in the French raids on Newfoundland in 1696, suggested that the road from Heart's Content to Placentia was perhaps not so good as the road between Paris and Versailles.

Remote northern U.S. roads weren't much better. As late as 1910, the road out of Silver City, on the south side of Lake Superior, was so rough that carriage horses dropped dead on it and passengers routinely tied themselves into their seats to avoid being pitched out. An early automotive visitor to the Canadian Prairies, Thomas Wilby, insisted that he encountered rain-filled potholes so deep that he had to take soundings before crossing them.

By the early years of the 20th century, the legendary disgrace of Canadian roads had evolved into the raw material for national mythmaking. Thomas Wilby encountered some of its worst aspects, the archetypal gumbo story—Wilby called it the mudman story—in 1912: A man walking toward Winnipeg along a muddy road sees a hat in front of him. Stooping to pick it up, he finds, to his astonishment, that there is actually a head underneath it.

"What are you doing here," he cries, to which the head answers, "I'm walking to Winnipeg."

This story, combined with a few cold winters and several stiff drinks, takes on a host of permutations until it reaches a more sophisticated version. This time, a fellow is riding a buggy through the gumbo. In front of him, he sees a hat moving slowly along the middle of the road, bobbing up and down. At great risk to himself, owing to the danger of being mired, he moves closer to the object, grabs it, and lifts the hat up high. To his horror, he sees a human face, moving steadily forward, the mud parting at its throat and leaving a brown wake as the head pushes forward. Before he can recover from the shock, the head turns to him and snarls, "Give me that hat, d'ye hear? I only take it off to ladies!"

"But what on earth are you doing here?" cries the man.

"Can't you see I'm riding horseback to Winnipeg?" snaps the head.

For millennia, the roads of Canada were made of water, which seemed to suit everyone just fine. Even the ambition to build roads across Canada is somewhat baffling. For decades, the North West Company managed to transport the entire peltry of the Lake Athabasca region more than 3,000 miles east to Montreal with no roads at all, relying for the most part on canoes constructed after the original Native design. The Hudson's Bay Company accomplished similar feats with a dizzying array of canoes, barges, bateaux, York boats, Albany boats, Red River boats, and Swan River boats, each watershed yielding a unique and specialized watercraft.

It is reportedly possible to cross the entire width of Canada without undertaking a single portage longer than thirteen miles. These portages count among the original Canadian roads, and anyone who has schlepped a canoe across even a short one knows they're every bit as discouraging as the miry carriage roads that early European visitors were forever complaining about. The Niagara portage encountered by the early fur traders has been dubbed the single most difficult portage in North America. Local Natives referred to it with a term that has been translated as "crawl on all fours." It could not have been significantly worse than the twelve-and-a-half-mile portage connecting the Clearwater River with Lac La Loche in Saskatchewan. In 1778, this remote and gruelling path was one of the busiest "roads" in Canada.

Admittedly, any trans-Canadian route that involves no single portage longer than thirteen miles would be an extremely loopy one that would take forever and leave the traveller with a high probability of getting lost and of losing his astrolabe—or his cellphone—on the way. In 2000, a twenty-one-year-old McGill student, Ilya Kivana, kayaked his way from British Columbia to Newfoundland in a single paddling season, something no one had done before. "The key," says Kivana, "is travelling light."

Travelling light or not, the fact that it can be done at all suggests how the prevalence of an ever-present waterway, requiring no taxation or work crews, worked against efforts to get down to the serious and extremely expensive business of hacking out and maintaining the immense roads across Canadian soil. Road-building initiatives were further weakened by the hysterical explosion of railroad construction that took place in the 19th century and left a great deal of Canada wrapped in a wide-ranging spider's web of iron.

The need for a trans-Canadian road was first sounded in 1859 by British Columbia governor James Douglas. Douglas had made his first of seven crossings of the Rocky Mountains as a twenty-two-year-old and during his career would range up and down the western coast from Russia to Mexico and back again. It was said of Douglas that he did "not much like the idea of being assassinated," a genuine threat given that he was disliked by the First Nations of the Northwest for insisting that they give up the practice of slavery. Douglas himself was part black, the child of a Creole mother and a Scottish father. In 1858, he wrote a letter inviting 600 black immigrants, mostly former slaves from San Francisco, to form a community in British Columbia, which they did.

In 1862, he implemented a scheme to build an eighteen-foot-wide wagon road 400 miles in length to service the gold miners of the Cariboo rush. This road, surely one of the wildest and most vigorous highways ever built, carrying fresh eggs and domesticated cats, as well as champagne and pianos, became a conduit of the frontier itself.

Pauline Johnson took this road, chaperoned by her squire and coach driver, "Cariboo Billy," who also served as her doorman and ticket taker. In one mining stop, he put up a marquee that read, "Whites A Dollar—Indians Fifty Cents." When a customer objected on the grounds that he was *half* white and *half* Indian, Cariboo Billy gave it some thought and, in a grand moment of

Canadian compromise, answered, "Fine, seventy-five cents!" which apparently left the customer entirely satisfied. Pauline Johnson gave her recital, danced until dawn, climbed

back into the coach, and set off for the next mining settlement. This new road took her into a prototypical Canadian society, one that was flying by the seat of its pants and where the rules of civil and even racial intercourse were getting made up as the game was being played.

This is likely not what the staid and frugal governor of British Columbia had in mind when he set out, without authorization, to borrow £100,000 to finance the road. It was in the throes of this road-building enthusiasm that he first committed to paper his notion of a transnational highway, one that would extend "the whole way from the Gulf of Georgia to the Atlantic." It was the early 20th century before such enthusiasm was expressed again. This time, the enthusiasts were without exception auto hobbyists with their own agenda, and it was not until 1949 that the government began to give it serious thought, and not until 1970 that the project was finally finished.

In the interim, the appearance of the "benzene buggy" would make the march of the 104th Regiment of Foot an odd bit of military nostalgia, reduce the Canadian rail network to a series of snowmobile trails and bike paths, and ensure, at last, the supremacy of the modern *rad*.

ON FRIDAY THE COMMON ENEMY, THE AUTOMOBILE,
GOT NEXT TO A COW ON THE EAST RIVER ROAD,
BROKE HER UP SO BADLY THAT POLICEMAN CHISHOLM
HAD TO DESTROY HER.
—EASTERN CHRONICLE, NEW GLASGOW, NOVA SCOTIA,
JULY 1907

UP THE CREEK WITHOUT A HORSE: THE ARRIVAL OF THE "RUNNING STINKER"

The first gasoline-powered motor car constructed in North America was cobbled together by Charles Duryea, an inveterate tinkerer who had grown up on a farm in Illinois and began his career, like so many early carmakers, repairing bicycles. At first, and for a few years to come, the local populace was unimpressed with his horseless carriage. Common opinion was that the only thing missing from the horseless carriage was a horse, and the only purpose they saw in it was to scare the daylights out of colts, kill innocent people, and run down far too many chickens.

Duryea's contraption, weighing 750 pounds and possessing two forward speeds and one reverse, rolled out of a barn in July of

1892. On its test run, it managed some twenty-five feet then, with a few adjustments, it cleared 200 feet. This new machine, which Duryea called a motor wagon but which other people were quick to call a motorcycle, was viewed with enough suspicion for it to be included in Barnum and Bailey's circus in 1896, where it joined a long tradition of such reputable freaks as the bearded lady, the Hindoo snake charmer, the Feegee mermaid, and, of course, Jumbo the elephant.

Two decades before this, a different type of horseless carriage had made its appearance on a Canadian road. Essentially a steam engine mounted on a buggy, it was the brainchild of Henry Seth Taylor, a jeweller and watchmaker. At its less-than-stellar debut in 1867 at a local fair in Stanstead, Quebec, a steam hose exploded, covering the vehicle and driver in a cloud of smoke and leaving the machine to be pushed home. After a few modifications, the vehicle managed to crash at the bottom of a hill, making it, in the minds of some, Canada's first car accident. Taylor's steam-driven carriage, which finally made it to the back of a forty-three-cent Canadian stamp, omitted two features considered essential to today's automobile: a steering wheel and brakes.

And a year before that, Father Antoine Belcourt, the parish priest in South Rustico, Prince Edward Island, had arranged for an American-made steam-powered motor wagon to be shipped by sea to Charlottetown. He demonstrated the machine at the parish picnic, where it crashed through a fence and rolled over, making June 4,

1866, in the minds of some, the true date of the first known traffic accident to take place in Canada, even though Canada wasn't yet Canada and Prince Edward Island was still

seven years away from travelling "the road to Confederation." It seems the parish priest abandoned his automotive career at that point, and local lore has it that the steam engine was removed from the car and used more productively to pump water before finally being melted down in a wartime scrap-metal drive. The machine did manage to outperform Taylor's contraption—by exactly two cents, later appearing on a forty-five-cent Canadian stamp.

The first automobiles appear to have been not so much *invented* as constructed, laboriously, piece by piece, in the face of considerable indifference, in the spare time of the mechanically minded. These ingenious fixer-uppers were experts at bicycle repair or the complex working of timepieces. They knew the fluidity of the near-soundless motion of the bicycle, the interconnecting cogs, the clasp and release of precision-machined gears, and the versatility of a thin rubber bladder inflated with air.

As for what to do with these machines once they were finished, their creators did not seem to know, or particularly care. From the time it was loosely invented to the time of its total domination of the road, four decades of automotive confusion ensued in which it was not exactly clear what, if anything, a car was *for*. Primarily, it was for a lark—a circus freak touted by Barnum and Bailey. By 1896, for the not inconsiderable sum of four dollars, it was possible to rent a car by the hour out of the Cyclorama building in Boston, the way you might rent a sailboard or go up for an hour in a hot air balloon.

It was in this manner that Canadian George Foss gained his firsthand experience of automobile travel. Even though the battery of his rental died after half an hour, he was impressed enough that, at the age of twenty-one, he constructed and demonstrated the first Canadian-built gasoline-powered car, the Fossmobile, as it was later called. Built in one winter, it was capable of fifteen miles per hour and a match for any of the hills of Sherbrooke, Quebec. It was the only such machine that George Foss would ever build, and it was a significant improvement over its Canadian predecessors, boasting gears mounted on the steering column and an engine housed not under the seat but in the front of the car, which was a great relief to the backbone. Foss said modestly of his machine, "It worked just fine."

Like Henry Seth Taylor before him, it never seemed to enter Foss's mind to mass-produce his car, or even to sell *a few* of them. When the president of the Eastern Townships Bank offered to put up the money for a production line, Foss said he would think about it. But instead his mind wandered elsewhere and he continued to build model train engines from scratch, casting the parts himself and later disassembling them to build something else, forgetting entirely about the banker's idea. It was, he admitted later, "my first big mistake."

His second was turning down the offer of a man who wanted Foss to invest in a company the fellow was trying to get off the ground. "There was something about him," Foss later wrote, that would make him "hard to get along with." The man was Henry Ford and his company the Ford Motor Company.

Foss, who did not built another car, sold the original Fossmobile for seventy-five dollars, and from then on contented himself with a back seat in the auto business, becoming a car salesman and eventually the owner of a high-speed car wash in Montreal.

He died in 1968, two years before the completion of the Trans-Canada Highway.

Even Henry Ford and eager bankers could not make the car, in Foss's mind, anything but a distraction and a source of amusement. A common first use of the fledgling technology was at fairs, automobile shows, parades, and gatherings. The races were not always with other cars, and not necessarily on roads. In 1907, four Toronto sportsmen took a modified automobile out on the ice of Toronto Harbour in a race against the ice schooner *IT*, which boasted a 500-square-foot sail. The twenty-five-horsepower auto held its own and the vehicle powered its way to the finish line slightly ahead of the schooner, in what a reporter called "the most sensational race ever seen."

Even in the face of such spectacles, the marginal position of the automobile was coming to an end. In Toronto, two inventors had assembled an electric-battery-driven two-seater named the Featheringstonhaughmobile, after F.B. Featheringstonhaugh, one of the inventors. His partner, William Still, patented a lightweight battery, and in 1899 a Toronto dye company bought a Still-powered delivery van with a range of thirty miles and capable of speeds of between three and thirty miles per hour. The motorized vehicle had accelerated beyond the fairgrounds and freak shows and was now delivering commercial goods on downtown city streets.

With the car's appearance, the unproblematic road was about to become an extremely contested site. Spaces where oxen once moved blithely forward, where children played road hockey, baseball, and games of their own invention, were about to become death traps lined on one side—or both—by the distinctive limiting wall of automobiles parked bumper to bumper. Posted over top of them would come the soon-to-be familiar signs reminding children, or at least their parents, that the provincial Highway Traffic Act makes playing games illegal on all provincial streets. What was once happily enough public space was about to be transformed into the exclusive domain of the automobile and the automobile owner, resulting not only in the criminalization of childhood play but in the origins of the children's park and playground, spaces made necessary by the full surrender of the public road and other public playways to the automobile.

Those accustomed to animal-based transportation didn't submit to this outrage without at least some grumbling about it. Reaction was the loudest in rural areas, although anti-automobile associations were springing up across the continent for the purposes of "self protection" and "restoring," as a New Jersey chapter put it, "our rights to the free and reasonably safe use of our public roads." The Farmers' Anti-Automobile Association of Pennsylvania produced a set of guidelines recommending that cars travelling at night "send up a rocket every mile, then wait ten minutes for the road to clear." The association allowed that the automobilist might proceed, "but with caution, blowing his horn and shooting off Roman Candles, as before." Should the automobilist encounter a team of horses—which he or she was very likely to do, given that in the early years of the 20th century the U.S. was home to fourteen million horses—the driver was to pull over immediately and promptly cover his vehicle with a blanket. This blanket was to be coloured in such a way as to "blend into the scenery." If the blanket did not blend, and if the horse still refused to pass, the automobilist was requested to "take the machine apart as rapidly as possible and conceal the parts in the bushes." In Vermont, where disgruntled souls had taken to stretching steel cables across roads in an attempt to impede the progress of the devil wagons, the state passed legislation requiring moving automobiles to be preceded by a person waving a red flag. Another local ordinance required the car owner to telephone ahead, warning the next town of its arrival—a case of using one suspicious new technology to protect ourselves against another one.

In Canada, popular reaction to the "benzene buggy" was equally dismissive. The PEI legislature banned automobiles outright until 1913, at which point they were grudgingly made legal for three days of the week. These "running stinkers," as they were sometimes called, were met with the same disdain that greeted the telephone, whose first users were mocked with the newly coined word *phonies*. In writing about the sudden appearance of "the gasoline devil" (or "devil wagon" or "chug-chug machine"), newspapermen and letter writers were quick to haul out the car-as-disease-metaphor—the automobile craze, the automobile fever, the "pleasure jaunters" addicted to their "fun," etc. Whoever these people were who drove these things, they weren't farmers. They weren't the plain, staid, predictable, hardworking, censorious lot who were suspicious of the city, the people who lived in the city, and all the things wickedly newfangled that the city was forever bringing forth. They were a moneyed but not necessarily youthful elite, and until the papers could discover a way to cash in on them, automobile drivers, on the pages of the newspaper at least, would be treated with considerable contempt.

In Nova Scotia, anyone desiring to drive a devil wagon had to first file his or her name with the Provincial Secretary and pay a fee of two dollars ("We wish it were 200," opined the *Eastern Chronicle*). "The Chauffeur," as the driver was called, was also required to fasten to his clothing a three-inch badge ("We wish it were as big as a board on a cow's face," further opined the *Chronicle*, in a cryptic reference that pointedly predates the car). In the *Chronicle*, those staid and reassuring men who drove horses were honoured as businessmen on legitimate business excursions, while the reckless joy riders in their running stinkers were out for the odious purpose of "fun." "Has the whole country, *whose people built the roads for their own use in order to do their work,* to put up with these life endangering pleasure jaunters?" thundered the paper.

The answer was yes, of course, but the editorialist had hit on a problem that has plagued the Canadian road since Anna Jameson's carriage was sinking in a slough of despond: whose responsibility is it to pay for the damn thing? The trucking industry, whose vehicles inflict the most damage on the road? The automotive industry, whose products cannot exist without the road? Or the poor schmucks lined up bumper to bumper on their way to and from work?

Since it was unable to squeeze or even legislate the useless and effeminate benzene addicts off the road, the *Eastern Chronicle* tried to content itself with a series of recent municipal laws prohibiting the use of the auto on Saturdays and Sundays. The top speed of a stink wagon was legally set at twelve miles an hour in the "village," and fifteen miles in the "country" ("Once again the countryman gets it in the neck," observed the paper). The town clerk of Digby, Nova Scotia, posted a notice to "automobilists" requiring them to continuously sound their horn when approaching and passing "any person driving, walking or standing on the street." Failure to do so resulted in a $30 fine or sixty days in jail. If the driver of an oncoming team of horses held up his hand, the "chauffeur" was required to bring his devil wagon to a standstill and remain that way until the buggy driver gave another hand signal allowing him to continue. The benzene buggy, it turned out, was a particular menace to women and children, as it was assumed that no female seated behind the reins of a horse could negotiate her way past an oncoming running stinker, although it was generally conceded that very few men could either.

The proliferation of the stink wagon proceeded at such a rate that road skills had to be acquired fast by any man or woman who still dared to drive a horse and buggy. In 1904, Ontario boasted 535 cars. Twelve years later, the number had increased to well over 50,000. By 1911, Canadians could order an automobile from the Eaton's catalogue and, if they didn't like it, get their money back with no questions asked. In 1916, the Canada Year Book conceded that the motor vehicle was the most important means of transportation in the country. Essentially, they were admitting that in the course of twenty years, two centuries of locomotive habits had been dislodged by the running stinker. By the 1920s—the first decade to see a reduction in the number of horses in Canada—British Columbia was issuing a licence that cost a dollar, required no examination, and thoughtfully advised motorists to use their vehicle's lights "at night." By 1928, the Canadian road system was carrying more than a million and half registered vehicles.

Never any great shakes to begin with, the Canadian road would undergo serious scrutiny over the next several decades, resulting in observations similar to the one made by Thomas Wilby in 1912:

that anyone wishing to tour Canada by road would be wise to suspend their car from a balloon.

=| |=

A looming question about the early road was which side to drive on.

The problem of right- or left-side road passage is as old as the Romans and, like much road history, was influenced by armed conflict. It is assumed that, in feudal societies, nearly everyone travelled on the left side. Since most people are right-handed, left-side passage was preferred by swordsmen, who wore their scabbard on the left and could thus keep their fighting arm closer to an opponent and eliminate the chances of knocking into people with their equipment. Up until the French Revolution, the aristocracy drove their carriages to the left, forcing the peasants to the right. During the revolution, in an effort to disguise themselves, aristocrats began joining the common folk on the right. A keep-right rule introduced in Paris in 1794 mirrored legislation passed in Denmark in 1793, the year that Alexander Mackenzie was making his 220-mile grease trail trek through the Rockies.

The first laws to regulate one side or the other road passage date back to the Chinese bureaucracy of 1100 B.C: "The right side of the road is for men," states the *Book of Rites*, "the left side for women and the centre for carriages." Dynastic rulings had more to do with protocol than preventing accidents, and people who have thought about this matter seem to agree that no good reasons exist, at least no good *technical* reasons, for either a right-hand or left-hand preference in road driving. Sometimes the decision is made on a whim, as in Burma in the 1980s, when dictator and former postal worker Ne Win decreed overnight that the Burmese people would now drive on the opposite side of the road—with predictable results. In the United States, the reason given for right-hand road passage is the fact that the British drove on the left. It has also been suggested that travellers with handguns transported their gun in the hollow of their left arm and travelled to the right, putting them in a better to position to shoot anyone who happened to be coming their way. Fear of ditches may have also had something to do with right-hand driving. Another technique of road driving, that of sticking to the middle of the road and thus avoiding the ditches altogether, has given us the modern acronym MOR. The introduction and widespread use of the Conestoga wagons in 1750 in America gave added impetus to right-hand driving: Drivers rode the left wheel horse or the "lazy board" at the left side of the wagon, leaving the oncoming left lane more visible.

The difficulties involved in getting comfortable on your own side of the road increased considerably when local and often abrupt decisions were made to switch sides. On a Sunday afternoon in April 1923, legislation came into effect that required drivers crossing from New Brunswick into Nova Scotia to get over to the other side of the road and stay there. As a result of the change, the Nova Scotia Tramways and Power Company complained that it was necessary to switch all the doors to the opposite side of its streetcars to prevent passengers from exiting out into traffic and sued the provincial government for the cost of the changes.

The "drive to the right" movement also put a great deal of pressure on local oxen. Described in 1912 by Thomas Wilby as "absolutely steady under automobile fire," the oxen could not be trained to get in tune with the new drive-to-the-right philosophy and were slaughtered to make way for a new generation that could. In Lunenburg County, Nova Scotia, 1923 came to be known as "The Year of Free Beef." Very quickly, the road was transforming from a site that was populated largely by animals into a space where animals were not only unwelcome but exposed to life-threatening collisions on a regular basis.

The arrival of the running stinker also posed another problem: Where were people going to drive them?

(5)

IT MUST BE CONFESSED THAT ON THE CANADIAN ROAD THE
CAR IS NOT YET A WELCOME DICTATOR.
—THOMAS WILBY, 1912

LITTLE DICTATORS

On August 27, 1912, a REO four-cylinder motor car (named for Ransom Eli Olds, who had made the first Oldsmobile) chugged down a Halifax road and ceremonially proceeded, tire-deep, into the Atlantic Ocean. After receiving its ocean baptism, the crew, consisting of British author and road promoter Thomas Wilby and his crack mechanic, twenty-four-year-old American Jack Haney, filled a flask with several fluid ounces of Atlantic Ocean water and set off to do something that no one had done before and would not do again for eight years: attempt to drive an automobile across Canada. As for the vehicle itself, it featured wooden spoke wheels, two speedometers, a single centre lever control for the gears, pedals for both brakes, and a horn that worked by foot. "I knew her for a beauty," wrote Wilby.

A verbose, opinionated, and witty English snob, Thomas Wilby had previously crossed the United States in the same manner, and the resultant book deal was incentive enough for him to try again, this time north of the border. In undertaking this expedition, he pioneered what would soon become a Canadian rite of passage: the cross-Canada car ride, with its gruelling marathon dimensions and its stunning shifts in scenery. Today, this journey is expected to entail a personal and psychological dimension in which the traveller comes back richer, somehow, and wiser. Wilby, however, like so many of the early British travellers, had enough wisdom already, thank you, and undertook his journey not so much to learn as to put his own preening intelligence on display for readers back home.

In fairness to Wilby, he was also one of the first practitioners of a new literary tradition, the book of the automotive voyage—what we now call the road book. In such books, the passage of the miles is undertaken at the frenetic speed of modernity and, as in the earlier canoe and carriage versions, chance encounters with rustic and inferior characters form an odyssey in which author and reader are shown to be better educated, more cultured, and generally a notch above the locals, no matter how colourful they might be.

By virtue of being the first person to drive a car across Canada, Wilby also scored some literary firsts as well. "The machinery split the hush of the solitudes with its deafening clatter." This sentence now reads like a cliché from a journalist's kit bag, but for Wilby it was the sound of a new age—a sound that was about to become more familiar and more prevalent than silence itself—and he was among the first to describe it. On favourable roads, there were times when his automobile "would shoot like an arrow," making Wilby among the first to link the new technology to the language of projectiles and weaponry. He also encountered some of the strange circumstances that beset early drivers: not only the dogs but the *horses* that chased cars out of sheer curiosity, or the experience of driving backwards for many miles, in reverse, up steep hills. Wilby covered a great deal of Canada driving backwards. At times, Jack Haney would get out and blow into the fuel pump in an effort to increase the pressure on a nearly empty tank. At night, Haney ignited the acetylene headlamps by hand. On the Prairies, their automobile plowed through a plague of gophers that got caught up in the wheels, clogging the axles and bouncing off the hood. At least once on the Prairies, they found it necessary to fill in the muddy road with wheat sheaves.

As he set off through the Nova Scotia landscape, Wilby observed that the local roads possessed the "consistency of batter pudding." At Truro, he washed down some reasonable sandwiches with what he called "a deadly concoction of stewed hay that masqueraded under the name of tea." In happier moments, beyond Parrsboro, he encountered sections of road "as smooth as a Shrove Tuesday pancake." Driver, mechanic, and long-suffering right-hand man Jack Haney noted more tersely in his own diary, "Bum roads most of the way . . . Bad culverts and holes."

Despite the thousands of miles that lay in front of them, there would be no windshield time between these two men. Wilby refuses throughout his book to mention his mechanic by name, and even insisted that Haney refer to him as "sir." Less than a week into the trip, Hanley noted in his diary, "Heartily sick of my companion. Will be mighty glad when the trip is over."

For Wilby, who remained oblivious to the feelings of his disgusted companion, driving on these roads induced what he called "a feeling of joy at the conscious bounding into infinitude"—one of the earliest attempts to describe the pace of the motorized road. In it, we hear the excitement of a man who feels himself a vital part of progress, even if he is travelling at a pace that barely keeps him abreast of the dogs that give chase to him. It is also an expression of the unencumbered tourist, the man at play, the "joy hog," as British traveller Robert Byron described the tourist. It is hard to imagine Alexander Mackenzie "consciously bounding into infinitude" as he set out to haul himself step by step on a 220-mile trek over the grease trails of the Rocky Mountains, laden down with seventy pounds of supplies, plus rifle and ammunition.

Wilby set out not so much driving west as being *driven*, for like many of the early cross-country motorists in both Canada and the United States, he left the actual means of transportation up to the hired help. He also had an agenda, a racial one, and perhaps one slightly more coy than the one expressed in his virulently racist anti-Mexican tirade (written with the assistance of his wife and published in the same year as his Canadian road book), which abounds with nefarious Mexican "greasers" determined to overthrow the U.S. government and take innocent white women to bed. His expedition also lacked what, until a few years earlier, no serious traveller in Canada would have ever gone without: a Native guide.

After two centuries in which the "Red Man" had been exoticized in the European imagination, fuelled a line of book publishing, and proved profitable as a tourist attraction and crucial as a guide, circumstances had changed for the worse. By 1912, a wide-ranging consensus among Europeans held that the Native was on the verge of extinction through death and assimilation, a belief that engendered a romantic and sympathetic view of the "Redskin." This sympathy waned significantly once it became clear that the Native was not only *not* going extinct, but was in fact still around, still having babies and now beginning to exchange "authentic" Indian garb for "store-boughts." For a readership trying to reclaim a vestige of what it hoped was its authentic and untamed former self, this was the greatest betrayal of all, and Wilby, like many of his contemporaries, had nothing but scorn for the modernized, adaptable, and unvanished Red Man.

Part of Wilby's intention with his trip was to close the European book on the North American Native and present to his audience the new, disappointing, and less-than-noble savage. At one point, near the banks of the Old Man River in Alberta, Wilby saw a group of Peigans dressed in black "store clothes," with their squaws, as he called them—nondescript creatures doing the laundry. "Pocohantas with a laundry," he observes gleefully. The great Hiawatha himself had become a patron of the "old clo's Jew." With this observation, Wilby, like Henry Ford, also forges an unfortunate link between the automobile journey and anti-Semitism. He also seems unaware that Longfellow's *The Song of Hiawatha* was itself a romanticized construction of the North American Native, pandering so successfully to European longings for the genuine that tourists to North America had already voiced their disappointment with the Red Man for not living up to Longfellow's portrayal.

The passionate Noble Savage that centuries of publishing had embedded in the Old World imagination was gone. In its place was a dreary race of people who did their own laundry and bought second-hand clothes from a Jew. This is the story that Wilby wants to tell: that the time for writing poetry about the Native is over. Modernity, as embodied by the road—in particular the trans-Canadian road he forcibly argued for—has won. The Native has not withstood the challenge and has become inessential scenery that passes by, sitting there, in Wilby's words, idly dreaming "of the buffalo's return."

Even as scenery, it turned out that the Red Man was not entirely profitable. In 1936, promoters of a trans-Canada highway—which despite being thirty years away from getting built was already being described as the "Highway of Hope"—were eager to rehabilitate the Canadian Native and return him to some sort of useful economic function as a tourist destination for the newly motorized America. Promotional brochures promised potential drivers along the soon-to-be-built Trans-Canada an opportunity to see the new, updated, harmless but still picturesque Natives: "Indian Camps are scattered across the Highway . . . These camps belong to the Ojibeway, a good natured, liberty-loving and illiterate people."

For both Wilby and the promoters of the Trans-Canada Highway, Indigenous peoples were to be looked at and photographed in the manner of scenery. That they allowed themselves to *be* photographed was, in Wilby's mind, proof of their debasement. That they would undertake this shameful activity "to the tune of a quarter in the palm of their hard brown hands" put them beyond the pale. The Red Man, sighs Wilby, "is being tamed to modern uses," and with this gloomy pronouncement, he hops back into his auto and hurries off to the more important stuff—such as tea. Wilby is faintly amusing about what Canadians see fit to call tea, "a deadly brew of senna and hay, boiled up for a second time after standing a year." In one Canadian restaurant after another, the poor man is forever fishing dead flies out of his teacup.

Wilby was also quick to engage in the already long tradition of smirking at the vulgarity of the local Canadian inhabitant, and the Canadian restaurant or inn did not fare much better. At times, he reaches a near-exquisite snobbery, a tour de force of put-downs made more slighting by subtlety: "The lady caller passed the time exchanging light and cheap badinage with a gentlemen visitor... [while in another corner] stood a whatnot littered with hoary literature." Wilby at once spots the "light and cheap badinage" and it is clear this "lady caller" and "gentlemen visitor" have not fooled him a wink. He knows what they're up to. And that "whatnot" in the background contains not just literature but "hoary" literature. He is alert to the distinction, and he wants us to know it. What he doesn't know is that in a few years his own book would also be "hoary literature" littering the top of a whatnot, while his other books would be considered, if at all, racist rants.

As an educated man touring Canada in an auto in 1912, Wilby offered up only the cultural assumptions of his age. Those assumptions change, and today the kind of wild and adventurous road travel that Wilby was undertaking is broadly assumed to transform the traveller. To a large extent, that is why we undertake it in the first place: to reposition ourselves against society, ourselves, and even our destiny. Wilby had situated himself in an ideal spot to be, among other things, the first to anticipate or least speculate about what would soon become a potent symbol of the Canadian road: the Native roadblock, that simple and symbolic demonstration by which the ceaseless, crucial, frenetic motion of a nation is brought to a complete standstill. Instead, each leg of his journey substantiated what he already wanted to see: "the finely alert Anglo-Saxon," whom he is pleased to watch disembarking from an immigrant ship, and "the brutish-looking peasantry from the Continent of Europe," whom he is decidedly unpleased to see disembarking from an immigrant ship. As Wilby drives across the nation, he doubts that even the vast character-building tracts of western Canada can make "good enlightened citizens out of the dregs of social Europe."

In the road, Wilby saw everything that was positive about the Anglo-Saxon character, insisting that the road was the moral muscle that would lift a man, and even a woman, up to the stature that the British Empire required of a person. The good road, insisted Wilby, "has reformed the man, reformed the housewife, transformed the children." The very family unit itself had been purified by better roads. How this has taken place he doesn't say, but he is insistent on the subject, insistent that our "race," as he puts it, has a divine destiny, convinced that the small town, not the city, will lead us to it—towns like Moosomin, which, he notes, "is barely large enough to contain its name."

Without roads, a town is like "a man without a head, or a blind astronomer," states Wilby. Give the Canadian farmer a good road, and he'll shave more often. Everything that is good, beneficial, even soul-enhancing, is a result of new and improved Canadian roads. At times, he reaches weird J.M Barrie–like heights, an unlikely Peter Pan yearning for a road system so modern, so complete, that in old age, "We may be able to travel, perhaps motor through Child Land, and enjoy again the primal simplicity and naiveté of that fair world of wonder and illusion."

In Wilby's time, no automobile had managed to make its way north of Lake Superior, and in yearning to go there, Wilby identified one of the great moral functions of the road: to take us to places that are uncontaminated by the greed of man, a place where we will experience regeneration and rebirth. A road to Lake Superior, Wilby insisted, would take us "up there." Once we have arrived "up there," we can experience the "wild beautiful places of theatrical beauty [that exist] *to renew our spirits and give us back ourselves.*"

The belief that by looking out car windows into "wild beautiful places" we will somehow be renewed and respiritualized is a long- and widely-held assumption of what the road will do for us. The road is now marketed this way, as a route into regeneration that connects one idyllic campsite to the next, lined with club moss and bunchberries, taking us to a place where the kingfisher makes its distinctive elongated dashes along the shore and the landscape is enchanted by the ghostly cry of a loon. Wilby, whether he knew it or not, was one of the Canadian road's first great marketers. But in selling the road, he exposed the essential paradox of the road. Every new highway allows us to escape from our tired selves, to leave the masses behind, to enter that redemptive space of solitude that we seem to hold in such esteem. Yet that same road also opens up that solitude to the chamber of commerce, the purveyors of the twelve-inch hot dog, the reporters with their microphones, the legitimate and illegitimate offspring of Tim Hortons, and the investors who will waste no time in constructing a spiritualization theme park with luxury suites, hot tubs, and wireless Internet connections in those same pristine locations that are supposed to "renew our spirits and give us back ourselves." It is a paradox that poses few problems to contemporary marketers. North of Superior, I once turned on the car radio long enough to hear an ad shilling a housing complex. "All the nature you need," sang a cheerful voice. "Plus the comforts of home."

=| |=

Thomas Wilby was only the first in a sequence of well-connected and accomplished men to cross Canada by car. He was followed in 1920 by Percy Gomery, a bank manager, president of the Vancouver Auto Club, and later president of the Canadian Authors Association, where he bitterly decried the lack of interest Canadians showed in Canadian books. His journey began in Montreal. Gomery, to his credit, did his own driving. He also brought his wife, an arrangement that would be embraced by many later cross-Canada automobilists.

There is something in a long road trip that endears it to the couple. The passage of shared time and places—the tasks, the monotony, the eventual breakout into the glory of the mountains or the daunting and impossible dimensions of the St. Lawrence River—mimics what happens in a long relationship. A road trip, like a marriage, goes on for a long time, perhaps too long, and is often both breathtaking and tedious. Both are more enjoyable when shared with the right person. Detours, rockslides, and treacherous curves are encountered, and sometimes a stranger is brought on board to alleviate the tedium or to help with directions. At times, the road is washed out entirely. In the act of travelling this road, through the effort and perseverance that puts all those miles behind us, we achieve a country, and each other. Those delightful hours and days of windshield time when even our silence is eloquent become the bedrock of a relationship, the shape of love itself: long and sinuous.

Gomery does not muse on the subject. Nor does he think to offer up his wife's name. None of the ensuing authors who took a wife across Canada with them could bring themselves to give the woman a *name*. They exist like reassuring pillows, sitting next to the driver/author, serving as receptacles for a sort of sheepish manhood in which a woman's innate rightness on all matters moral and ethical is sighingly conceded. Gomery comes closest to individualizing his road partner, even giving her the moniker "the skipper." Her name was in fact Bernadette, a glorious name that recalls a different age when train travel was common and in the rural regions of the country it was not unknown for automobile owners to grease the axles of their vehicles with bear fat. West of Ottawa, we find her sitting alone in her husband's hopelessly mired car, draped in mosquito netting, clutching an umbrella and revolver for protection against the bears. When help arrives, she is revving the engine in an attempt to scare the bears off. This is one of the first appearances of the female on the Canadian road, and, not surprisingly, it is a damsel-in-distress narrative in which the woman is allowed and even expected to display some pluck but in the end the heavy lifting gets accomplished by the men. In the

United States, things were somewhat different. Women had been quite cheerfully crossing their country on highways for some time, and writing books about it as well.

Gomery was followed in 1926 by the indefatigable Dr. Perry Doolittle. Today, Dr. Doolittle is known, if at all, as the father of the Canadian Automobile Association, the ubiquitous CAA, an organization that now boasts nearly five million members. A proud-looking, fine-featured fellow with owl eyeglasses and the obligatory potent moustache, he embodied a host of late Victorian virtues and was the first physician in Toronto to make the rounds of his patients on a bicycle, then the first to make them in an automobile.

Doctors, in fact, were originally the most enthusiastic of the new road users, happily taking their medical skills to the patient. With the mass marketing of an affordable automobile, the trend was reversed and the sick and dying were expected to take their ailments to the doctor at the hospital and, eventually, to pay criminally high fees to park there. Despite gaining a reputation as the "King of Canadian Roads," Doolittle is little known today—just another of the faceless, pavement-grey gentleman who worked unfailingly to make the Canadian road network a reality.

Dr. Doolittle was also one of the very few men modest enough to *not* write a book about his crossing. This seems an odd oversight by a man eminently positioned to do so, and one who had already written a book about the joys of Canadian bicycling, back when a bicyclist was known as a "wheelman." Doolittle was a founding member of the Canadian Wheelmen's Association in 1882 and

himself a champion racer. But instead of
writing a book about his road trip, he
teamed up with an American filmmaker,
Edward Flickenger, chief photographer for
the Ford Motor Company and a man who
would ally himself with several Canadian
projects of dubious worth.

    It was the film footage of Edward Flickenger that helped cata-
pult the American-born, Canadian-raised fake conservationist, anti-
Semite, and nut bar Jack Miner to fame. "Wild Goose Jack," whose
stated ambition was to "fill the whole room with heavenly bread
right from God's own oven of love," is sometimes thought to have
been the first man in Canada to band birds. He *did* band birds, but
refused—despite being begged to do so by the Canadian government—to place any data on the bands other than scripture. At the
behest of Henry Ford, Flickenger filmed Jack Miner's bird "sanctu-
ary," providing Jack with footage that he used during his later lecture tours. In these talks, the "Father of Conservation" stood on
stage dressed in his red plaid trousers, playing the morally superior
country bumpkin who disseminated the racial assumptions of his
age. He loved to make jokes about Injun Joe and his "squaw."
"Everybody think like me," he mocked. "Everybody want my squaw."
He told "Ikie and Jakie" stories: "Mister, I don't look like so much,
but I make lots . . . my cheque is good for 75,000." His bizarre self-
published writings promote a theory in which the Native North
American, in allegiance with the "drowsy-eyed Jew," are conspiring
to rid North America of its wildlife. The thesis is a knock off from
the *Protocols of the Elders of Zion*, published, promoted, and perpetrated in North American by Henry Ford's foundation.

Dr. Doolittle's involvement in this network of hate is not clear. It is known that he drove 4,794 miles (7,715 kilometres) from Halifax to Vancouver in a spanking-new 1926 Ford Model T in forty days while suffering only four flat tires—a remarkable achievement, considering that the entire country possessed only a few hundred miles of paved road, and most of that around the cities. Dr. Doolittle rather cleverly brought along a set of flanged railway wheels, which allowed him to drive on the train tracks. In the absence of roads, he did this for some 800 miles. Wilby, on the other hand, had simply had his REO speedwagon plunked down on the ties and jolted his way over them. Unlike Doolittle, who had arranged rail clearance in advance, Wilby had agreed with Jack Haney that should a train come during their night runs on the rails, they would leap to safety and sacrifice the vehicle.

As the King of the Canadian Road, Doolittle was intractably convinced that the highway was first and foremost a moneymaker. This belief was the founding pillar of the Trans-Canada Highway movement and of nearly every road ever considered since. Nowhere do these early boosters mention construction or maintenance costs, medical costs due to accidents or WVCs (wildlife–vehicle collisions)—let alone ungulate–vehicle collisions (UVCs) or elk–vehicle collisions (EVCs)—the cost of clearing the animal carcasses from the road, the cost of signage, or even the cost of salting or sanding winter roads, removing graffiti from the rock cuts, or "road administration" (roughly four percent of total road expenditures). No financial downside is admitted to the road at all. The entire Canadian highway network, it seems, would be kept and maintained by an army of patriotic automotive volunteers, all of them wearing leather gauntlets and long, dashing scarves. In Doolittle's era, this might have been a fair assumption.

Outside his car, the landscape Doolittle experienced was essentially the same as that of Wilby's trip thirteen years before, though somewhat more denuded of trees. It is easy to forget what a blasted vista Canada was back then, not a land of trees but of tree stumps, of mine tailings and rivers clogged with sawdust from the mills. By Doolittle's time, it was also further stripped of any meaningful Native presence. Neither his speeches nor film footage admit to the existence of First Nations people, an Aboriginal past, or any past at all beyond Longfellow's *Evangeline*. The Canada he envisioned was a tabula rasa on which the great Presbyterian virtues could be writ large. The good doctor was in such a hurry that he more or less skips any mention of central Canada and the Prairies altogether; it is just the Maritimes, then Quebec, where he sees fit to compare French Canadian society to a gathering of chickens. "The priest is the benevolent autocrat of his little parish," he writes, "and when there is a sign of a hawk they all flock to him like chickens to the protection of the mother hen." From Quebec, he is then on the other side of the Rockies.

Doolittle, along with Wilby, are among the first of the modern men to promote and finalize the "playground theory" of Canadian wilderness. Until the appearance of the automobile and the roads to support them, this concept was hardly thinkable. Radisson and his First Nations colleagues, starving to death on the south shore of Lake Superior, did not view the North as a playground. They observed that the Native women they travelled with were so hungry they had "become barren and drie like wood." They did not think twice about eating the beaverskin diapers belonging to Native infants, "even where the children beshit them above a hundred times." When the diapers had been eaten, they ate their tents until their gums bled, and when their tents were eaten, they starved to death, and with regularity. A century after Radisson, during a brutal winter, the fur trader Alexander Henry entered a small clearing in the bush to come upon a human hand staked next to a campfire.

The transformation from a place where people ate each other's hands to Canada as Playground is one of the more remarkable promotional manoeuvres perpetrated on a nation, and is intimately connected to the road. In his 1926 address to the Empire Club, Dr. Doolittle proclaimed that the entire province of Nova Scotia had become "a natural playground ... a wonderful covert for wild game and a delightful playground for the summer tourist." Hunting, fishing, and the lesser practices of relaxation and spiritual rebirth were parts of this playground as well, and there was just no end to it. "What are the Rocky Mountains," asks the doctor, "but fifty Switzerlands rolled up in one?" Dr. Doolittle, to wild applause, finished his address to the Empire Club with a reading of a poem by Conan Doyle:

Through the years that care to be
the mighty voice of Canada will ever call to me.

═╣╠═

Despite the insistent east–west pull, there is another way to cross Canada: north to south. In the writings of Black Elk, the north–south road is the true road, the "Red Road," created by the Great Spirit and given to the red people. It is the equivalent of our "straight and narrow," beginning in the south at the source of life and proceeding into the purity of the North.

True road or not, this particular overland voyage had decidedly few takers, the most intrepid of whom was Alaska's famous sourdough, Slim Williams, a walking, occasionally driving promotion for the Alaska highway.

Provided with a letter of introduction to Alaska's Congressional delegate in Washington, and offered 300 dollars to attempt the journey, Slim left Copper Center, Alaska, on November 21, 1932, with a team of eight dogs, one of which was eaten by wolves between Telegraph Creek and Hazelton. During a particularly difficult stretch, Slim endured illness and snow blindness and nearly drowned. He traversed mountains so high that they were, in his words, "upendicular."

After six months of sledding, he traded in his conveyance for a wrecked Model T Ford for the dogs to pull, camped in city parks, and signed autographs. He arrived on September 16, 1933, at the Century of Progress fair in Chicago, pitched his tent, and for six weeks became part of the Alaskan exhibit. Despite a visit with the U.S president, he failed to initiate any real interest in a highway to Alaska. In 1939, Slim, now fifty-seven years old, tried again, this time on a 300-pound motorcycle, which he often resorted to pushing and dragging all the way from Fairbanks, Alaska, to Seattle, Washington, again to no effect.

=╪=

The first cross-Canada road trip to travel exclusively on Canadian roads took place in 1946 when Canadian Brigadier R.A. Macfarlane, DSO, plopped the rear wheels of a brand-new Chevrolet into the Atlantic Ocean at Louisbourg, Nova Scotia, and set out on a much-publicized car voyage across the country. With military efficiency, the brigadier, who knew a great deal about tanks, crossed the entire country in nine days, arriving in Victoria, British Columbia, where, to front-page fanfare, he and his companion were awarded the A.E. Todd Gold Medal for keeping his vehicle on Canadian soil throughout.

Another military man to hear the mighty voice of Canada calling to him was the formidably named Nicholas Monsarrat, a high-ranking British civil servant and author of, among other books, *The Cruel Sea*. In 1955, Monsarrat undertook to drive across Canada with nothing but his unnamed wife, "a few old clothes, a camera, a fishing rod, a pair of binoculars," and what he debatably describes as "an inquisitive mind." He also had the good fortune to be driving a Bentley Mark VI Continental provided by Rolls-Royce Canada and capable of hitting speeds of 120 miles (nearly 195 kilometres) per hour.

Monsarrat, himself a solid convert to the playground theory of Canada, had some work to do squaring his vision of unspoiled nature with the vulgar reality of the Canadian roadside circa 1955. On driving west out of Toronto, he warns his readers that to spend time on this stretch of road means acquiring a taste for fried potatoes, ice cream, frozen custard, bowling, and above all the twelve-inch hot dog.

Although Monsarrat doesn't pursue it, the relationship between the twelve-inch hot dog and the Canadian road is as old as the paved highway itself and provides an approving nod to anything that is larger than it should be—a boast that the old prehighway eight-incher is no longer good enough. It is also resembles the road in that it keeps getting longer, costs more money, and can carry nearly anything you want on top of it. Presumably, Monsarrat wouldn't be caught dead eating a hot dog, twelve-inch or otherwise, and his prickling at the vulgarity of the Canadian roadside is diplomatically constrained and marked by a damning with faint praise.

For all its democratic possibilities, it has been the fate of the prototypical Canadian highway to be travelled almost exclusively by towering snobs. Monsarrat's book, *Canada Coast to Coast*, is an embarrassing little affair accidentally printed with the cover upside down, and so obscure that it doesn't even appear in any of the author's later bibliographies. It serves no purpose except a hasty attempt to gird the author's reputation, which had recently grown gargantuan with the release of the film version of *The Cruel Sea*.

In *Canada Coast to Coast*, Native Canadians are once again swept off the road, off the landscape, and resolutely off the pages of the book. Monsarrat, in search of what he calls "an unspoiled natural paradise," finds it in the Lake of the Woods region, and here, aside from references to "superstitious Indians," and "Indian tribal warfare," is encountered the book's only mention of the

Aboriginal people of North America. Monsarrat insists that a whining outboard motor is "every Indian's proudest possession." Here he contributes to the formulation of the new racism sounded by Wilby and others. For centuries condemned as a savage, now the Native is condemned as not savage enough.

There are traces of wit and stylistic economy in the book, and there is Monsarrat's genuine love of the sea and the seafarer, a rich tradition against which today's smoothly paved road still cannot compete. At Georgian Bay, like so many long-distance Canadian drivers in 1955, he proceeded on a two-day, 542-mile boat journey to western Canada by boarding the SS *Assiniboia* north of Barrie, Ontario. Monsarrat, a seaman, allows his eye to travel lovingly through that ship, to "the oak panelling" and the "flowers set in wooden buckets." The author of *The Cruel Sea* was now in his element.

Monserrat had arrived in Canada in time to witness the splendid intersection between the water voyage and the road trip. The golden age of Canadian travel was still in evidence around him. Waiting to ferry cars and passengers were grand steamers with names like the *Noronic*—which tragically burned at anchor in Toronto—the *Assiniboia*, the *Huronic*, and the SS *Milwaukee Clipper*. Throughout their panelled interiors, porters carried ice in buckets and passengers danced to a string orchestra. Advertisements placed in the Ontario Motor League Road Book urged motorists to "Save 240 miles of congested highway driving." To compete with the informality of the modern road, passengers were even invited to "dress as you please."

More than a half-century ago, my mother-in-law stood at the passenger wharf at Sault Ste Marie with her one-year-old baby in arms, frantically waving to the stern of the *Huronic* as it pulled away, her car, her family's clothing, her husband, everything she needed already on board. The captain, after some deliberation, turned the ship around and picked her and her child up, insisting that this was the only time in his long maritime career he had ever done so. No doubt it helped that my mother-in-law was then twenty-four years old, with dark hair that swept below her hips, and was holding a baby, but nonetheless, overcoming the practical difficulties involved in turning around a ship that was considerably longer than a football field and returning to pick up a passenger speaks loudly of the chivalry and the conventions of long-distance travel in mid-20th-century Canada.

It is in this golden age that Monsarrat's heart lies. He recounts yearningly how the *Assinboia*'s captain once counted on Lake Superior 150 vessels within sight of his own ship. Those days had already faded—a way of travel entirely deep-sixed by the running stinkers. There were several decades of glorious coexistence to be had, however, and Monserrat was lucky enough to have caught the tail end of it.

Despite the speaking engagements and the spanking-new Rolls-Royce, Nicholas Monsarrat was also a man with a dirty secret. One of the reasons that *Canada Coast to Coast* reads like a corporate press release is that for many years Monserrat had been a press officer for the British High Commission in Pretoria, where he performed the role of chief apologist for the apartheid regime of South Africa. In this capacity, he had a dubious role to play in a dubious story: the virtual imprisonment of Seretse Khama, heir apparent to the chieftancy of Botswana's largest clan, and the white English woman whom he loved and married, Ruth Williams. After enlisting the bishop of London, the colonial office, and the London Missionary Society in a failed attempt to stop the marriage, the government of South Africa persuaded British authorities to lure the couple out of South Africa and back to England and to keep them there indefinitely. Their union was viewed as so calamitous that the plane carrying Ruth Williams was rerouted to ensure that it did not fly over any "white" areas. Amid all this deception, the shadowy skills of Nicholas Monsarrat came into play. It was Monsarrat's job to keep other members of the press and the public unaware that Botswana's favourite couple were being hurriedly exited to the British Isles. This he did in exemplary fashion. The riots, the murders, and the brutal punishments that took place in Botswana as people demanded that their leader and his wife be returned to them make no appearance in Monsarrat's little book.

Instead, he spends half a page uncomfortably attempting to titillate the reader with a story about young women in Toronto who, he is convinced, are in the habit of standing above newly constructed subway grids in the hope of having their dresses blown into the air. This is a far cry from young Lieutenant Le Couteur's obvious respect for the sixteen-year-old girl who calmly put a boat hook into the eye of an attacking bear, and Monsarrat's passage is a torturous piece of innuendo in which "young girls . . . stand there in blank astonishment . . . their skirts billowing. Or am I being naïve?" he asks.

It is hard to say exactly what Monsarrat is being. He was peripherally involved in one of the greatest love stories of the 20th century and did everything he could to sabotage it. He drove a luxury automobile across an entire continent and cast everything he saw around him into the rigid contours of what he thought was his own objectivity. He fawned over Stratford, Ontario, because it had, well, *Shakespeare*. He made tired, predictable comments, and then he went away.

The road permits this superficiality, even encourages it. There is something about gazing out the window of a fast-moving automobile that facilitates a great deal of surface, surface, surface, but very little depth. We become a land-based version of Herman Melville's sailor, "for sailors only go around the world without ever going into it." At no time does Monsarrat ever seem *of* the road, of motion and transition, that constant, timeless state of not-knowing and ever-changing that the road offers. There are roads that knock our personality into bits and allow us the freedom to start again. Monsarrat was not in search of anything like that. He wasn't a lover; he was a peeper. He did not carry the proper baggage that the road demands, and to the road he gave nothing.

Nor did Monsarrat have anything to say about the road itself. To him, it was a means for the consumption of scenery, of getting to a destination. He does admit that the long journey across the Prairies, while boring, is no more boring than a long sea voyage and, like the sea itself, there is a rhythm to it. This is his only attempt to experience the road as something *in* itself, as a physical reality that tempers our relationship to time.

In 1963, eight years after Monsarrat's pleasure jaunt, Toronto-based academic and writer Edward McCourt became the last person to cross Canada in his car and still manage to wrangle a book deal out of it. Like Wilby, Doolittle, Gomery, and Monsarrat before him, his book furthers the disappearance of Native people from the Canadian landscape, replacing them with quotations from Shelley, Keats, Pericles, Sibelius, Vita Sackville-West, and Lytton Strachey.

An irritable crank, an aesthete, a critic, and an intellectual unflinchingly armed with the confidence of a powerful education, McCourt had no use for a Canada that allowed its children to play baseball, or any other game that did not fit into his framework of the illustrious European classics. His long drive was not a search for anything, certainly not a new identity—he was exceedingly pleased with the one he had—and certainly not for the essence of the country whose roads he and his wife were travelling. He viewed the trees and forest in particular with horror, despised camping, and was desperately in search of anything that resembled his darling Europe. The local and the indigenous were of no interest to him. His method of experiencing his country was to take a Canadian locality and give it legitimacy by writing about the celebrated European personage who happened to have spent some time there. The further he drove into Canada, the further away from Canada he got. He did, however, share Lieutenant Le Couteur's interest in young women, keeping his eye especially peeled for those who happened to be "pretty, neat, and well-painted."

Then there are Newfoundlanders, and Newfoundland women, who bear the brunt of his scorn for producing too many babies, a character flaw that he blames on a fish diet and the baby bonus. A great deal of his book is spent giggling over the baby bonus and complaining about children. McCourt cannot drive by a child without making some sort of contemptuous remark, leaving the reader to wonder what his unnamed wife made of all this.

He also manages to drive across the entire province of Quebec, quoting a great deal of Thoreau but without speaking to a soul or giving much indication that the province contains anyone who speaks the French language. As for that language, McCourt insists that it is not a language at all, at least not "a vital living" one, but just a mere symbol of "a deep-seated resentment." Even Thomas Wilby's quietly suffering mechanic, Jack Haney, had the good grace to note, with some astonishment, that "everybody is French. I can't understand anything they say." Wilby admitted there was such a thing as a French-speaking Canadian and described him as an "old-fashioned, English-language-murdering, tobacco-growing, semi-literate, easy-going, badly dressed antique." McCourt saw sights of great historical import and was keen to drone on about them, but he was keener yet to ogle the girls on Dufferin Terrace. "They know why Eve was created and they walk in that knowledge," he winks. Quebec, it turns out, is entirely filled with hot Catholic girls who "wear shorts" and "have the gleam of the devil in their dark eyes." It doesn't seem to occur to McCourt that the gleam might be in his eyes as well.

The paved road, with its access to the swoop and speed of the 20th century, has now made it possible for erudite authors to dismiss an entire people, indulge in a metaphysical examination of the sexual wiles of young French Canadian women, and smear French Canadians as "volatile . . . acquisitive . . . resentful . . . and superficially charming."

In this respect, both McCourt and Wilby fall prey to one of the great dangers that swift movement over considerable distances poses to the traveller, especially the traveller armed with a book deal. The danger is the very act of observation itself, an activity that takes what's in front of us, in all its breathtaking and confounding variety, and reduces it to "scenery." Human beings are reduced to "characters" and required to act like characters by saying things in a folksy dialect that the writer can then spell phonetically for the amusement of his readers. Edward McCourt is hardpressed to find such subjects and falls back on that old reliable standby, the local drunk. In the Maritimes, he calls up a worse-forwear fellow clutching a paper bag to his chest and manages to elicit an appropriately folksy saying: "Every time I get married," the man says, "I buy a new pair of shoes."

Confident that he has fulfilled his writerly obligation by capturing something authentic, McCourt is pleased to continue on his journey. He remains, however, acutely disappointed at not finding Bloomsbury-type bon mots being tossed off at local Canadian gas stations. After giving the matter some thought, he decides that the reason there are no "folksy characters sitting on benches, logs, stones, etc," is because they are all off getting interviewed by the Canadian Broadcasting Corporation.

With this remark, the author of *The Road Across Canada* pinpoints what has increasingly become the default function of our news and cultural agencies: the desperate search for something authentic, the compulsion to get out there and photograph, interview, or write about something, anything, that is genuine. Weirdly, in a country where four out of five of us now live in a city, the assumption persists that the authentic must, for some reason, be rural and remote.

With his heart and mind set on the great civilizations across the ocean, Edward McCourt had no expectation of finding anything of value on the Canadian road, and as a result, he doesn't.

As McCourt travelled, he made constant note of a type of cultural and even linguistic contamination that followed in the wake of the highway—the "sleazy" tourist shops and the desperate, high-stakes tourist marketing that turned the North into "a playground." Suddenly, every community that the road passed through had become a "Sportsmen's Paradise." To achieve this status, all a town needed was "a pond, a duck or two, and a Chamber of Commerce." Today, arguably, not even the pond or the duck are mandatory.

In *The Road Across Canada*, McCourt also contributes enthusiastically to the eradication of the Native presence from the Canadian landscape and, more importantly, from the Canadian story. The Native is noticeably removed from the main highway and placed deep on the back roads, leaving only a few shabby tourist stops to sell a much-reduced facsimile, and not even a reasonable facsimile, but a copy of a facsimile.

In reading McCourt's unproblematic road trip, the reader gets the sense that the entire country has been quietly and peacefully ethnically cleansed. There are no powwows, no powwow stadiums, no First Nations, no Native history, no lacrosse, no blueberries, no Native languages. Instead, there are witty quotations from Boswell and erudite critiques of denominational education, but there are no Ojibwa, no Mohawks, no Cree, no Sioux. There is only Sitting Bull's rifle, which, McCourt gleefully assures us, is a fake. This eagerness to reveal the Native as fraudulent is a carry-over from the Wilby era and reflects the discomfort that McCourt encounters when even peripherally attempting to deal with "otherness."

There are also no black Canadians in McCourt's book. The road he travels does not enter the neighbourhood of Africville, a 300-year-old community of former slaves that had evolved into a suburb of Halifax, Nova Scotia. Three years after the publication of *The Road Across Canada*, black Canadians would be removed from their homes—some in garbage trucks provided by the municipality—and relocated into a grim housing project so that Africville could be turned into an industrial park. It seems impossible for Edward McCourt to take this road, or to even know it exists. It strays too far from a road that is bordered by his own privilege and the comforting murmur of the editor's office and the faculty club. *The Road Across Canada* simply cannot go there.

There are other places he has difficulty negotiating, the Quebec Bridge, for example, or, as he terms it, the "great" Quebec Bridge. Thirty years earlier, the good Dr. Doolittle had called it the "greatest feat of engineering in the world," a statement that reveals the tortuous doublespeak of the highway booster.

The Quebec Bridge was an engineering fiasco and arguably one of the worst-designed bridges in the world. It collapsed twice in less than ten years and stands as a mournful tribute to greed, vanity, and cost-cutting. When it collapsed in 1907, seventy-five men died.

The vast majority of them were Mohawks, experts in high steel, from the Cauhnawaga region. Fifty years after it happened, the

Mohawks of Quebec and upper New York State still referred to this collapse as simply "the accident." It is hard to imagine a Mohawk family on either side of the border that did not lose a husband, a father, or a brother in that catastrophe. In 1917, it fell into the St. Lawrence River again, and this time eleven men died. The rumour still

persists that engineers, upon graduation, are fitted with a ring cut from the steel of this bridge; a physical reminder of the engineer's responsibility, and of the consequences of incompetence.

Wilby, Gomery, Doolittle, Monsarrat, and McCourt have nothing to say about any of this. McCourt has great fun mocking the Indian maiden, as he calls her, for forever throwing herself into a waterfall, but he can't bring himself to mourn the scores of Native skywalkers who fell into the water and died doing a job that few other men were capable of, whose lives were lost because a high-ranking American architect couldn't admit he had made a mistake, and who, in forfeiting their lives, made it possible for McCourt and his wife to drive in blissful ease from one side of Canada to another.

In a few short years after McCourt published his book, the highways of Canada would become a transformative space. The next generation was about to take to the road in a rite of passage that would see them symbolically enter their country and, for the first time, attempt to imaginatively possess it as a place distinct from Europe, or even the United States. For at least one generation, to *not* hitchhike across Canada was almost unthinkable. To *not* stand outside of Wawa for interminable hours, to not fall in love between Brandon and Moosimin, to not evade the interest of one or more sexual deviants, was to be condemned to a staid, indoor existence that was downright un-Canadian and to exist in a kind of perpetual childhood. As with Mingus and his fellow poets swarming across the country decades later, they positively demanded, begged, that the road change them. It went without saying that a long road trip could only make better poets, and better people. For McCourt, Wilby, et al., the road was not conceived as a transformative opportunity at all. These men came out exactly as

they went in. The road was a conduit to spread their superior in-
tellect and breeding to a scattered people they considered to be in
desperate need of it. Their books stand as testaments to themselves
exactly as they were and always would be.

==⊨

Just as we enter Quebec City by crossing the Quebec Bridge, we also
reach Northern Ontario by crossing a bridge; this one spans the
French River on what is now called Highway 69. This bridge has
never been boosted as a great architectural wonder, nor, to my
knowledge, has it ever collapsed. Wilby crossed this bridge, or at
least its predecessor, and so did McCourt, who acknowledged the
existence here of a "splendid picnic-site." Everyone who was anyone, he noted, had passed beneath here on their paddle to the west.

For centuries, every trade good, every pork-eating paramour
who had a sweetheart waiting for him in Rivière-du-Loup (and an
Ojibwa girl at Bawatang) passed through this spot. So did every
English adventurer eager to write a book or to put some distance between herself and her drunken husband. The pressed skin of every
beaver, mink, marten, and wolverine purchased by the North West
Company passed between the walls of this narrow gorge. Radisson,
barely old enough to shave, floated through here on his way to
make first contact with the northern tribes, his mighty appetite
sated by a bowlful of human flesh. With him was his brother-in-
law, Des Groseilliers, still shaking from his last epileptic fit. Champlain, the birdwatcher; Jesuits on their way to be disappointed, to
die lost in the woods; the devious and doomed Etienne Brûlé;
Simon Fraser; Alexander Mackenzie, troubled by unsettling visions

of the dead; McTavish, the McGillivrays, the whole penny-pinch-
ing brigade of ruthless Scot entrepreneurs passed repeatedly
through this bottleneck of the first trans-Canada route.

It was here at this spot, with her golden hair showing beneath
her bonnet, that English-born painter Frances Anne Hopkins was
serenaded by the songs of the voyageurs. From her seat in a canoe,
she made enough sketches to paint her arresting and photographic
Canoe Manned by Voyageurs Passing a Waterfall, one of the most reproduced images in Canadian art.

The granite wall forming the background of that painting is the
same wall we see in front of us when we park the car and get out
to look around. The sweeping gallantry of the paddler as he reaches
down for the white lily pad to present to the female traveller depicts the heartfelt mythos of the voyageur. It speaks of the search
for love and beauty that lies entangled in the long miles of travel.

Frances Anne Hopkins painted this canvas in 1869, by which
time the world had witnessed its first automobile casualty and the
horseless carriage had already begun crashing into the fences of
rural Canada. She died in 1919, having lived long enough to not
think twice about stepping into an automobile herself. This transformation happened in less than a lifetime. She went from those
gallant voyageurs who picked her up bodily each time they landed
and carried her to shore to prevent her boots from puncturing
the canoe, to the running
stinker that "split the hush
of the solitudes with its
deafening clatter." While
she was at her easel, painting those exquisite details,

the auto was running roughshod over the livelihood of her favoured subjects. The annihilation of fur-bearing animals and the common appearance of decked vessels on the Great Lakes had already shut the book on the voyageur and his method of travel. He was dead but didn't know it yet—a relic for the tourists to write about and for Mrs. Hopkins to paint.

The canoe du nord, the railway, the *Huronic*, the *Assiniboia*, all of it was preparing to disappear down a road that would not exist anymore. A new and brash traveller was about to take to the highways. Impatient with the romance of the past, he had no need for the Native peoples of Canada to guide him or to trap his furs or to prop up his sagging vitality. The land was mapped; the furs were trapped out. He needed only a stage on which he could demonstrate his shining self.

(6)

POKER BORES ME BUT I DO ENJOY EXPLORING.
—CHARLES BEDAUX, 1934

HIGHWAY TO THE MOUNTAINS

On May 25, 1934, Charles E. Bedaux made his small but lasting imprint on Canadian history when he announced to an assembly of Canadian newspapermen that he was about to undertake something that had not been attempted by a non-Native since Alexander Mackenzie in 1793: an overland journey from Edmonton across the Rocky Mountains and through to the Pacific Ocean. The announcement of this trip, grandly dubbed the Bedaux Canadian Sub-Arctic Expedition, was made, fittingly, in the plush interior of Montreal's Cloud Club. The feat involved driving five *autochenilles*—Citroën half-tracks—and fifteen tons of supplies across some of the world's toughest mountain ranges. It would result, or so Bedaux put it to a government official, "in scientific information which is to be placed at the disposal of the Canadian government."

This trip was just the latest in a long series of madcap schemes for Bedaux. As a delinquent French teenager, Bedaux had run with a wild crowd and fled to America in 1906, a twenty-year-old starting out his career in the New World as a "sandhog," pushing a wheelbarrow filled with sand during the construction of the great skyscrapers of New York. Within twenty-five years, he was a millionaire—the inventor, promoter, and chief beneficiary of the infamous and elaborate Bedaux "speed up system," a Frederick Taylor-like industrial time-management scheme that some said "squeezed the last drop of blood out of the worker." The unions despised him, while just about every important corporation in the world, from General Electric to Campbell Soup, bought wholeheartedly into his system.

In the whole vast grey phalanx of men whose steady measurements and methodical, dark-suited professionalism have resulted in the highways of the world, Charles Bedaux, or "Charles the Man," as his intimates called him, sticks out like a harlequin. After his brief stint as a sandhog, his career became a dizzying ascension into American-style success. He invented, or claimed to invent, a special toothpaste that doubled as an ink stain remover. He peddled life insurance in the Midwest, selling more policies in a month than other men sold in their lifetime. In 1916, he patented a device for timing the duration of telephone calls. There are claims that he invented the boom microphone to keep troublesome wires off the studio floor, eliminating the time workers spent tripping over them. He patented an improved car door. He stood at podiums and gave weird and esoteric public lectures, some of them attended by employees of the U.S. War Department, who presumed him to be a German spy.

Then, in 1929, in an almost incomprehensible undertaking, he became the first man to cross the Libyan Desert by automobile. The journey, which took place above the equator at the desert's widest point, began in Mombasa and finished some 9,500 miles later in Casablanca, making its way on a vast number of Goodrich tires—Goodrich being one of Bedaux's 600 clients. Such an expedition had never been attempted in a motorized vehicle before and perhaps forms the basis for *Car and Driver Magazine's* claim that Charles Bedaux invented off-road racing.

Five years later, in 1934, Charles Bedaux prepared his team for his grandly named sub-Arctic expedition. This team, more frequently referred to as an entourage, included a dental student, an Academy Award–winning Hollywood photographer, a Swiss skiing instructor, a French gamekeeper, an out-of-work bush pilot, several guides, geologists, wranglers, and cowboys, and Reginald Geake, a local loner assumed by his Canadian neighbours to be a British spy. The British Columbia government, unwilling to pay for its own surveying expedition, permitted their provincial surveyor to piggyback on the Bedaux expedition, on the assumption that Bedaux would pick up the tab.

On the morning of July 6, when the expedition set out from Edmonton's Hotel Macdonald, it did so in the Bedaux style, following a champagne breakfast and the gift of a horseshoe-shaped floral arrangement presented in the hope of bringing good luck. Locals on the ground knew that anyone attempting to crash their way over the Rocky Mountains in a collection of strange French-made automobiles would require as much luck as possible. Back in France, however, Andre Citroën himself had expressed complete confidence that his trucks would conquer the Canadian backwoods.

For a brief while, the expedition was accompanied by two limousines. Apparently, they didn't get far. Even before the trucks had made their way out of Edmonton, a hard and continuous rain had begun to fall. Bedaux, in keeping with his partiality for comfort under unlikely circumstances, had personally designed a tent that could be set up from inside the tent itself without the user ever having to get wet. Each Citroën half-track was provided with one. Even with first-rate gear and top-of-the-line automobiles, the going was slow: they made it fifty miles in eleven hours, to the town of Athabasca, with many of the men now dubious if not downright disheartened.

From Athabasca they travelled existing roads to Grande Prairie, where the local mayor speechified about his hopes that Bedaux's efforts would result in what he called considerable "materialistic advantages." Such advantages are widely presumed to be a logical byproduct of the road, or of merely *taking* to the road—the mayor was expressing a commonplace confidence that roads in themselves lead somehow, invariably, to wealth.

The first ten miles out of Grande Prairie took four hours. Heading for the Peace River Trail, the B.C. provincial surveyor, Frank Swannell, noted in his diary, "Bad roads cut to pieces in the rain."

The celebrated Citroëns were beginning to break down. Bedaux had already fired the nineteen-year-old dental student for his preference for flirting with local girls instead of crawling on his back beneath the half-tracks to repair them. At Fort St. John, Swannell noted that the main street had become a "sea of mud." On July 22, the party made eight miles, travelling a trail cut by Depression relief gang labour. By late July, the Citroëns were being dragged through swamps by the men. At this point, to move the trucks at all, the expedition was relying on corduroy roads that they themselves had to cut and build. The trucks, without a proper underpinning of roads beneath them, had proved almost useless from the start. At best, they were consuming a gallon of gasoline per truck for every five miles (eight kilometres) achieved.

On the banks of the Cameron River, Bedaux made the decision to abandon the Citroëns altogether and rely entirely on pack horses. There are indications that Bedaux knew from the beginning that the vehicles would be useless to him and had engaged them as a publicity stunt, and a means of gaining a powerful sponsor in André Citroën. Bedaux then gave 4,000 dollars cash to a nineteen-year-old trail hand, with instructions to purchase as many pack horses as he could.

Shortly after this, cameraman Floyd Crosby, who would go on to film *High Noon*, embraced Hollywood's nascent love affair with the car crash when he arranged to send three of the vehicles, loaded with empty boxes, toppling off a steep cliff into the Halfway River while he filmed the event. Frank Swannell noted in his journal, "Cars make a spectacular plunge, the empty boxes with which they are loaded spilling in all directions. Tremendous excitement, the drivers jumping out in all directions." A fourth car was sent downriver on a raft that was meant to collide with a cliff rigged earlier with dynamite. The dynamite turned out to be a dud, and eventually the raft and the Citroën washed up on the shore, where a local resident managed to salvage it. The vehicle proved useful for another two decades.

By August 14, the Bedaux Canadian Sub-Arctic Expedition consisted of three pack trains and at least three dogs, including a stray mongrel picked up on the Halfway River and dubbed "Halfway." In what seems like another Hollywood moment, more than a hundred horses, some of them mounted, forded their way across the cold glacial water of the Halfway River. On the other side, the riders found themselves in completely unmapped territory. Two weeks later, they were into the high Rockies. By September 4, they had reached a clear mountain lake, which Swannell, in his official capacity, promptly named Fern Lake in honour of Bedaux's wife.

On September 8, as the food began to run out, Bedaux opened a case of champagne. One bottle was broken, and the remaining eleven were shared by twenty-two people. This single case of champagne, rather like the miracle of the fish and the loaves, was to mutate, in the eyes of later critics, into endless cases of vintage French wines, proof positive that Bedaux was an idle dilettante at best, and probably a fascist spy.

With his weird expedition, Bedaux insisted that it was possible to travel in comfort and even luxurious style over the mountains. In this respect, he epitomizes what a great deal of Canadian road travel has for some time become: a long, comfortable passage during which the quietest of Mozart's sonatas can be played on the radio while we negotiate the sheer 200-foot precipices on the north shore of Lake Superior or vanish into a tunnel that burrows through the mountains of the Rogers Pass. Even though Bedaux himself was soon to be an entirely reviled figure, his modus operandi of minimizing the gruelling wear and tear of long journeys has become the norm of highway travel. Where earlier travellers packed a length of rope to tie themselves into their carriage seats, Bedaux packed a kerosene heater to ensure that his wife's morning bathwater was warmed to specifications.

Bedaux had changed the rules of the road, and especially the Northern road. The wealth that bought him and his travelling companions their comfort is now routinely engineered into nearly every kilometre of Canadian highway and every air-conditioned vehicle that scoots the surface of it. Today, this extreme level of comfort is taken for granted, but critics of Bedaux laughed at him for achieving it in a region of the world that they have long and romantically insisted demanded masculine endurance and harshness. Instead, he packed in tins of Devonshire cream, a wife, a mistress, and even a Spanish maid. He introduced women, and rather aristocratic ones at that, into the otherwise all-male preserve of the Canadian North, something his critics, Pierre Berton in particular, found unforgivable. He was also in the habit of hiring whatever local help he needed, often paying extravagant and unheard-of wages.

Although Bedaux managed some degree of comfort—and with his wonderfully named mistress, Bilohna Chiesa, providing the style—he failed in his objective to cross the mountains. By late September, hoof rot had begun to infect the horses and the men were shooting three or four of them every morning. Despite the champagne treat, morale was deteriorating: the oddball Reginald Geake, in a fit of annoyance with a fellow traveller's dog, picked up an axe and split the poor creature's head open. It is said of Geake that he had commanded a destroyer in World War I and that he met his demise shortly after the Canadian Sub-Arctic Expedition when he joined up with a blind man who possessed the power to telepathetically divine the presence of gold. Apparently, both he and his diviner were shot dead by bandits in the Sierra Madre Mountains.

At some point in the fall, Bedaux conceded defeat. He grandly announced his intentions to "present a report together with the data we gathered to the International Highway Commission with the suggestion that the route be considered. To my mind it is the only logical one." Bedaux had previously expressed some astonishment that the governments of neither Canada nor the United Stated had any stated plans to build a highway through to the Alaska region, nor saw any reason to do so. The failure of his expedition to make its final destination, he reasoned, was a fatal culmination of hoof rot, bad weather, and gumbo—the same jelly-like morass described twenty years earlier in Thomas Wilby's mudman story. Apparently, Bedaux was curious enough about the gumbo phenomenon that he actually sent a sample of it in a jar to be examined by French scientists. What the French scientific community had to say about the gumbo, if it ever arrived, is not clear.

Bedaux then disappeared from Canada, leaving behind the corpses of many dead horses and five abandoned Citroën halftracks, one of which is today on display in the Western Development Museum in Moose Jaw. From Pierre Berton to Bedaux's biographer, Jim Christy, to George Ungar's fascinating documentary *The Champagne Safari*, from *Canadian Geographic* to *Maclean's* and *Car and Driver Magazine*, each new decade sees a new retelling of the Bedaux story. Today, he is remembered on topographical maps of the west coast, courtesy of B.C. surveyor Frank Swannell, who named a mountain after him, Mt. Bedaux, which rises 7,555 feet into the air.

History hasn't shown any posthumous kindness to Charles E. Bedaux. His wild escapade into the Canadian Rocky Mountains has been roundly condemned as a quarter-of-a-million-dollar publicity stunt. The fact that the Alcan Highway, now called the Alaska Highway, follows some of the route chosen by Bedaux has not helped his cause any. To Pierre Berton, he was a hateful man—even less than a man, "a creature," a "fascist"—whose head wasn't shaped properly, and most damning of all, he was short; "a five foot six egoist trying desperately and not very effectively to be noticed."

Aside from being short and having an improperly shaped head, Bedaux was a collaborator with the Vichy regime, for whom he agreed to establish a utopian commune in Roquefort, France, where money was eliminated and replaced by something Bedaux called the Bex, a stable measurement of people's work ability. By this point in his career, Bedaux was the sole inventor of a philosophy that he called Equivalism, something he once described as a "communism within the form of capitalism," an idyllic union that entirely disregarded the fact that the world was at war. With his typically manic energy, Bedaux courted the Soviets, the Americans, the Greeks, the French, and even the German High Command, who responded enthusiastically to his scheme, first conceived during his Libyan desert trek, to build a pipeline across Africa that would deliver peanut oil into German-occupied regions. It is this scheme that allowed a New York writer to say of Bedaux that he was the only American to ever sell out his country, literally, for peanuts. That Bedaux had a softness for high-ranking people regardless of their dubious political inclinations was established as early as 1932, when he allowed Wallis Simpson and the former king of England to get married in a castle that he owned in France. A German sculptress later cast a bust of Bedaux that was exhibited alongside those of Goering and Hitler.

As the American Army advanced through North Africa, the man who attempted to drive a tractor across the Rocky Mountains was spotted on a terrace enjoying a brandy with a German officer and arrested as a collaborator and flown to the United States by American authorities. Although Coca-Cola and IBM and many other companies have been forgiven for trading happily and extensively with the Nazi regime, Charles E. Bedaux has not. His quick banishment from the more respectable pages of history was hastened by a dismal end in a U.S. holding cell above a Florida gas station while awaiting trial on charges of treason. In February 1944, shortly before a jury was to deliver its verdict on one of the

charges, Charles Bedaux, expressing his love for his wife and maintaining his innocence, swallowed a carefully hoarded supply of Luminal and killed himself.

WE WERE. . . PERFORMING OUR ONE NOBLE FUNCTION, MOVE.
AND WE MOVED!
—JACK KEROUAC, ON THE ROAD

THE ROADS MOST TRAVELLED

The Trans-Canada Highway was officially opened on September 3, 1962, in a ceremony attended by 3,000 people assembled in rare British Columbia sunshine beneath the peaks of the Selkirk range at the Rogers Pass. The event was marked by a certain unmistakable nervousness. The Saskatchewan representative began his speech by announcing what a pleasure it was for him to be in Quebec, and the B.C. Minister of Highways thanked God for the beautiful weather. "I want to thank God personally," he insisted, perhaps confident that his night job as a preacher entitled him to such familiarity. The province of Newfoundland pointedly refused to send anyone to attend the ceremony, and New Brunswick also took a pass. The premier of British Columbia would have nothing to do with the event, and the province of Quebec would have nothing to do not only with the event but with the entire highway. The commemorative five-cent stamp issued to coincide with the opening was marred by an embarrassing spelling mistake, and most ominously of all for a road long promoted as the bedrock of nationhood, the bus carrying the musical instruments of the Princess Patricia's Canadian Light Infantry band got lost on the way from Calgary and the ceremony was forced to open without a rendition of the Canadian national anthem. Ironically, the instruments did arrive in time to play "God Save the Queen" at the end, suggesting that this great road that was supposed to announce a confident nationhood was not as far removed from its colonial past as might have been hoped.

These mishaps were a reflection of the highway itself, revealing a dim comprehension of what this new road was for and what exactly people were supposed to do with it. Wisely, Prime Minister John Diefenbaker elected not to reiterate the Sioux interpretation of an east–west road as a "black" or "blue" road, a path of error and destruction taken by those who live for themselves rather than their country. Instead, he expressed confidence that this east–west highway would bring Canadians "closer together." He also voiced his heartfelt hope that the road would always serve the cause of peace and that it would "never hear the marching tramp of warlike feet."

Diefenbaker's aspiration for a road built in the service of peace was a new take on the Trans-Canada Highway. Twenty years earlier, a provincial highway minister had described the proposed Trans-Canada as a no-nonsense "all Canadian route for the transportation by road of military forces and supplies, and of raw ma-

terials from farm, forest, stream and mine to markets and facto-
ries." Other officials stressed the "urgent necessity of this road
from the point of military preparedness, tourist attraction and the
opening up of mineral wealth." All of these priorities differ significantly from Diefenbaker's spiritual framing of the highway and
echo the traditional belief that roads will both save us from the
enemy and make us rich.

Prior to World War II, the most commonly stated motivation
behind the construction of a trans-Canada road was the desire to
attract tourists, especially what was known as the American auto-
touring public. "We must give to the American tourist a system of
modern, dustless highways, over which it will be a delight for him
to travel," gushed the chief of the Dominion Travel Bureau,
preaching to the already converted members of the Good Roads
Association in 1941. These money-grubbing origins have undercut
all attempts to write the Trans-Canada into a glowing heroic narrative. How exactly does a country spin a tale of growth and national unity around a road whose very construction was based
largely on U.S. know-how and whose explicit purpose was to clog
itself with as many American tourists as possible?

It doesn't help that the Trans-Canada Highway was built grudgingly, over some sixty years. It involved much squabbling about
who was to pay for it; was started, abandoned, started again; and
lacks the unity of being a single thoroughfare, consisting instead
of a web of highways that have resulted in an astonishing number
of casualties and maimings. Commentators have tried to duplicate
the great railway narrative, providing heroic statistics in terms of
dynamite used, bridges built, stone removed, cost per mile, and
so on. They have tried to reduce the highway into a triumph of

engineering alone. But all of those facts and statistics have only served to diminish the road and what it means. Does it help us to know that in closing the notorious Lake Superior "gap," 2.73 million yards of rock were blasted and moved? When it is explained that the highway's most expensive section cost $319,000 a mile to build, have we really learned anything? One writer deliriously stated that, "If all the earth and rock used to build the highway were dumped into railway freight cars, the resulting train would be long enough to circle the earth five times at the equator." Imagine that. It is uncomfortably obvious that whoever penned these words didn't have the faintest idea what he was attempting to write about. The only value that is on display here is an abject grovelling to the gods of size and immensity.

Certainly there are facts concerning the construction and maintenance of the Trans-Canada Highway that are worth repeating and convey a sense of the significant engineering achievement that the road represents. It is not every highway that requires the regular firing of artillery shells to keep the traffic flowing. While many roads in the world require an army to keep them clear of bandits and armed political opponents, the Trans-Canada is perhaps unique in requiring an army to keep it clear of snow. The Royal Canadian Horse Artillery routinely fires off any number of eighteen artillery emplacements located in British Columbia's Rogers Pass to create small, pressure-relieving avalanches to dismantle disastrous accumulations of snow. The soldiers who fire these cannons take their marching orders from the local weatherman. The army had previously tried planting dynamite fired by remote control but abandoned the experiment after discovering that the explosives were being eaten by bears. The same muskeg that bedevilled the building of the transcontinental railway and helped doom the cross-mountain extravaganza of Charles Bedaux also presented unique engineering challenges to road builders. Test drilling in the Rogers Pass area revealed muskeg reaching fifty to sixty feet (fifteen to eighteen metres) in depth, and some sections of the Trans-Canada are built right on top of it.

Then there are the underground rivers. How are construction crews supposed to respond when, after opening up a section of a mountainside with dynamite, they are faced with a fierce and endless rush of water from a river that was previously buried? At the other end of the country, blasting undertaken during the construction of the Canso Causeway, which cuts across the deepest natural harbour in North America, is said to have cracked the basement of every house in the town of Mullgrave, Nova Scotia.

Despite the technical challenge of building the Trans-Canada, a retelling of the bald facts only stands in the way of a more meaningful mythologizing of the story. In a National Film Board production, *The Longest Road*, one of the rare documentaries that deals with the Trans-Canada Highway, there is considerable footage of exploding rock. We see no end of displays of confident, hard-hatted men in chequered shirts forever blowing up the sides of mountains. Unmistakably triumphant, these shots, each with an explosion followed by its cloud of smoke and lingering dramatic cascade of rock, becomes a visual representation of progress itself.

Such footage oozes with technocratic confidence and takes for granted that the highway is of remarkable significance, yet never bothers to demonstrate that significance, or even attempt to explain it. From encyclopedias to congratulatory websites to Centennial celebration coffee table books, the Trans-Canada Highway is subjected to a bloodless merging of science, economics, and patriotism that results in such pallid descriptives as, "The efficient transport of people and goods plays a vital role in the health of our nation's economy." Summations like this would make Jack Kerouac choke on his drink and baffle any Canadian who ever donned a backpack and stuck out his or her thumb as they took to what Gordon Lightfoot called in song the "carefree highway."

Despite the confident language of unity and progress in which descriptions of the Trans-Canada are couched, the meaning of the road insists on heading off somewhere else. To Lieutenant Le Couteur, a traverse across vast tracts of Canada was a golden opportunity to meet girls and test himself in battle. Thomas Wilby saw the road as a chance to expound the racial assumptions of his age. To Dr. Doolittle, it was a source of endless financial activity that would result in 5,000 American tourists each year, each spending at least ten dollars a day. Do the math, he advised. To the author of *The Cruel Sea*, it was an opportunity to peek beneath the skirts of the young women of Toronto and engage in a type of clipped corporate doublespeak in which great care was taken to offend no one while perpetuating the great racial divides. To the French-born American Charles Bedaux, the great highway was a means of bringing the world to him, a way of reaching out across vast areas with a new understanding, *his* understanding, a route by which he could attain the unconquerable heights of his own ego. Edward McCourt, who came late enough to actually *have* a Trans-Canada to drive, found in the highway an opportunity to display his own privilege, lament the sad ignorance of Canadians, and drive through a world that, without his knowledge or notice, was vanishing beneath his wheels.

Following its problematic opening on September 3, 1962, it was no longer just authors, highway boosters, and millionaires who could cross Canada, but anyone who had access to a car, or even a thumb. Young Canadians were now in a position to do what Americans had been able to do since 1906: cross their country from coast to coast without having to rely on a railway timetable (though they would be required to adjust their watches six times).

In doing so, they would have the distinction of travelling the longest continuous national highway in the world: at 7,714 kilometres (4,793 miles) long, the paved, typically two-laned thoroughfare requires two lengthy ferry rides to complete, bringing the total distance to 7,821 kilometres. Its builders subjected themselves to what they called the Ten Commandments, one of which stated that the driver will never face a curve of more than five degrees in arc. Another stated that the grades of hills will be maintained at six per cent, or no more than six feet of incline or decline for every 100 feet, and that sight distances will be maintained throughout at a minimum of 1,000 feet. It is the combination of these commandments that allows us to maintain a constant speed as we drive from one side of the country to the other. Such exemplary engineering standards have not always been the norm for the Canadian road; the Opeongo Line, a twisting and storied settler route connecting Ottawa to what is now Algonquin Provincial Park, was said to have been surveyed in such dizzying turns because it allowed the surveyor to move efficiently from one local whisky still to another.

The newly opened Trans-Canada would soon become *the* route

of the upcoming generation. Within a few years, young Canadians were getting in touch with the vagabond voyages of the poet and beginning their long journeys of discovery and rejection by hitching across Canada and into the mountains. By the time of Edward McCourt's crossing in 1965, the Trans-Canada was preparing to become a physical embodiment of the breach between generations and the physical setting where that conflict could take place. McCourt's exclusionary primness and unquestioned confidence in his own world view placed him securely on the previous side of the division. With his disdain for regional cooking and wilderness, he was already lying in the dust of Kerouac's "fine gone daddies," who, two decades earlier, had ball-jacked their way across America, stealing cars, "making" girls in the mountains, and "doing the monkey dance in the streets of life." They had been doing so since the late forties. The formal and tired rhythms of McCourt's *The Road Across Canada* sound the final few gasps of something that had come to an end. The next generation was already fleeing into the dreamy feedback of electric guitars, riding a new impulse of protest, restlessness, and discovery, and using the road to do it.

It was understood early on that the highway was perhaps the quickest route into the authentic. It takes the traveller forward to a place known vaguely as Somewhere Else, located at a distant spot far away from work and home, away from all that is accepted and therefore phony, or at least suspect. The open road lies in the opposite direction of school, parents, home, work, and the alarming dead end of something called adulthood. It takes us into a place of self-discovery. It is, in the U.S. at least, literally a freeway. Even if Canadians cling to the more royal *highway*, it still provided a generation with the opportunity to reject what they were convinced was in desperate need of rejection: the *pace* at which life was lived. Thoreau may have warned us that it was morally and aesthetically wrong for a human being to travel more than a hundred miles a day, but Thoreau was a stodgy crank who was critical of everything from the railway to the telegraph to the mail itself. Even the author of *Walden* was soon to be co-opted into the love of the open road. One U.S. motor enthusiast grandly equated the automobile with Thoreau's utopian cabin and termed long distance-road travel "Thoreau at 29 cents a gallon," equating the road itself with natural paradise.

To the young drug-, alcohol-, and jazz-fuelled characters who cram the pages of *On the Road,* hitchhiking a hundred miles for a pack of cigarettes, getting back in time to swallow a few Benzedrine tubes, and then get on with the all-consuming business of sex and poetry, was nothing at all. Nor was it any big deal to get in the car and drive 1,700 miles from Denver to Oaxaca, Mexico, to get a "quickie" divorce. Everything was suddenly quick. And everything was dissolvable, even marriage.

The paved highway was both contributing and paying homage to the altered pace of existence. The breathlessness of that pace defines Jack Kerouac's classic book of movement, unfolding with the startling speed of a jazz saxophone riff. Kerouac himself could type a hundred words a minute and found the act of removing a sheet of typewriter paper to be so slow and onerous that he typed *On the Road* on a single massive roll of paper—a medium that in the end actually came to resemble the road.

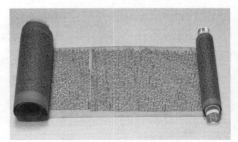

The sheer tedium of hitting the carriage return and indenting each new paragraph also proved too slow for Kerouac. As a result, fourteen days after starting his classic, he had one single-spaced paragraph that stretched 120 feet in length. "I wrote it fast," he wrote, "because the road is fast."

It is this insistence on speed and on upping the tempo at which life is lived that is still startling to a reader of *On the Road*. In each sentence, the book insists, even proves, that life as it was then was in dire need of rejection, or at least rethinking. With the completion of the Trans-Canada in the mid-sixties, a physical space had been created where this rethinking could take place. Canada was now in a position to have its Beat generation. In much the same way that Neal Cassady and Jack Kerouac set out across their country in search of the ultimate tenor sax solo, young Canadians set out as well, to a somewhat different soundtrack and for different purposes. Yes, they would do the monkey dance in the streets of life; they would strip their clothes off on a whim and run naked through the fields. They would search for kicks and excitement, perform all the ornate contortions that are required of the young in their rebellion against the old. Yet they would also seek the purity of the road, and by doing so, they would become pure themselves.

This is not something that can be confidently stated about the often sociopathic hustlers and drunken mystics who zoom through the pages of *On the Road* and seem more intent on destroying, or at least losing, themselves, "stumbling off the protective road where nobody would know us," as Kerouac puts it. In the end, it is not so much a place within their country that they're trying to find as it is a place *away* from their country: a place in opposition to suburban comforts, respectability, and a working life;

a place situated within the ecstasy of poetry and experience; a place, finally, within their *gang*, that musical litany of names— Oedipus Eddie, Sal Paradise, Dean Moriarty, Bull, Marylou, Babe Rawlins, Carlo Marx, Chad King—all those hard-drinking miscreant loser poets and deadbeat dads who form a substitute for their own failed families. In their mad dashes to Frisco, Denver, New York, and Mexico City, they carried as much luggage as Edward McCourt did, though it is a different type of luggage and comes out in a contempt for anyone who is old, or married, or homosexual, or intellectual, or holds down a job, or speaks "eastern college talk," or checks their watch to determine if they will make the next town in time. This disdain for even the loosely normal is a posture against insecurity and the fact that the very young haven't yet achieved anything to justify their confidence in their own superiority. Really, what they have done is take to the road in a quest for experience. The road *is* the experience, and the fact that it often takes place at high speed can obscure whether anything significant is taking place on it.

In the young, a frantic pace is perhaps a good thing in and of itself. But for those who are not young and have through the years established a pattern of memory and habits that have assumed shape, meaning, and even dignity, the pace facilitated by the highway did not necessarily lead to personal liberation but to the destruction of what was known and familiar, to the destruction of experience itself. Author Robert Kroetsch has suggested that the Trans-Canada has played a role in turning Prairie towns into ghost towns. The small towns that he grew up in were situated some ten to twelve miles apart, which meant that a farmer with a team of horses could haul a load of grain to an elevator and make it back in a working day. With the appearance of the highway, the need for communities to cluster close together dissipated and the space between towns expanded to some forty or fifty miles, allowing one town to flourish and another to decline. The means of measuring time and distance had been changed by the new pace of the Trans-Canada, and the previous logic of it displaced. Grain elevators also suffered from this change and by the late eighties were being torn down in vast numbers.

In British Columbia, a Native couple, the Walkens, knowing that the Trans-Canada was about to be built through Spences Bridge, B.C., started up a roadside motel and restaurant business in 1961. The Walkens were soon the biggest employer in a town that boasted a permanent population of 138. After twenty years of operation, however, the motel–restaurant shut down. "People got in too much of a hurry is what happened," suggested the couple's daughter. The distance between Vancouver and Spences Bridge fell neatly into the measure of one full tank of gasoline. This, in the early days of lengthy travel, was considered a reasonable day. Over the years, as gas stations proliferated, people grew accustomed to filling up again and travelling all night if they wished. Spatial logic was changing in response to the possibilities opened up by the new road.

=‖=

For all the bald boosterism promoting the financial benefits of the highway, the role of the road as a pathway for *material* goods holds little sway on our imagination. It is in the movement of artistic, emotional, and *social* goods that the road truly moves us. As quest,

as art, as ritual, the road take us further into the realm of imagination than it does into the land itself. Whether we travel the road
of life, go to Kansas City, or get our kicks on Route 66, there is no
end to the symbolic and narrative encounters with the highway.
We can hit the road or take to it; we can fear what lies around the
corner, for the road contains twists and turns that conceal what
lies in front of us. Roads are tortuous and can lead to dead ends.
We can get left on the side of them. We may be crowned King of
the Road or made to wear a crown of thorns up a road named Do-
lorosa. At some point, we will find ourselves alone in a dreary
roadside motel, playing solitaire and watching *Captain Kangaroo*,
or standing on a corner in Winslow, Arizona, with any number of
ex-lovers on our mind. Like Robert Johnson, we can get off at a
southern crossroads between Yazoo City and Beulah and sell our
soul to Lucifer in exchange for the ability to play guitar. We suffer
bumps, encounter roadblocks, eat the dust of those who move
faster through life than we do. We fear the road to hell and strive
for the path to heaven, or vice versa. We stand at celebrated corners—Portage and Main, Hollywood and Vine—but at some point
we take that long walk down Lonely Street after stumbling
through the boulevard of broken dreams. Some friends we trust so
much we'll follow them down any road. We drink and drug ourselves to excess and are forced to travel the long road to recovery.
And who knows? After getting off Lonely Street and travelling the
long road to recovery, we might even end up on easy street. We are
swept away on the information superhighway.

The language of moral, emotional, and psychological existence
is massively indebted to the road. "The road is life," wrote Kerouac. Without it, we could barely speak to one another. The pen-

etration of the road into our language and song is so comprehensive that it's difficult to tell where it ends or begins. The traversing of any space at all, whether it is moral space, temporal space, or characterological space, is a road. Change is a road. Sometimes, but much more rarely, even a road is a road.

By contrast, the railroad has left little behind in the great word hoard of the language: *the end of the line*, *riding the rails*, the rather feeble *all aboard*, and *choo choo*, which sounds not so much like a train as a facsimile of a train, a toy train. The road has quietly usurped the railway's position as *the* Canadian story, though it has not yet been granted its status, and just as quietly turned the train into a somewhat reduced stand-in for nostalgia. In the 1960s, the railway was greatly diminished when the decision was made to devote the Lake Superior North Shore line exclusively to freight traffic, preserving perhaps *the* most spectacular train view in the world for the exclusive enjoyment of freight containers and a handful of train engineers, while passengers were routed inland over the flat boreal plain of Northern Ontario. Today, brightly coloured cars zip past the great lumbering locomotives, and the car drivers flip an irreverent wave, press the accelerator, and are gone.

Early promoters of the Canadian highway, even early writers and thinkers, expressed little awareness that the highway would have an impact on the status of the railway. In the United States, however, American writers rushed to embrace the new freedom provided by the road and were venomous in their rejection of the train. As far as they were concerned, the train was a mechanism for social restraint, a stifling, hidebound holdover from the Old World. The train divorced the traveller from nature and the pastoral opportunity of the American West, and was crushingly impersonal, forcing passengers to witness the same scenery over and over again—and in the opinion of one female writer, stank of the bananas that were constantly fed to hungry children. The novelist Theodore Dreiser rejected trains as "huge clumsy unwieldy affairs, mass carriers . . . great hurry conveniences for overburdened commercial minds." In certain corners of American culture, the railroad has been given a decidedly tough ride. In the Western movie, a genre that celebrates the open trail, the railway and its backers are routinely portrayed as murderous, cold-hearted assassin–capitalists who will stop at nothing to clear the land for their corporate bosses. Ambrose Bierce, in his caustic *Devil's Dictionary*, published in 1911, defines a railroad as "the chief of many mechanical devices enabling us to get away from where we are to where we are no better off."

The road was a different matter. From Emerson ("Everything good is on the highway") to Walt Whitman ("Oh public road . . . you express me better than I can express myself") to Kerouac, the highway, with its intricate network of side roads, was seen as the true mirror of the American experience: impulsive, close to the earth, and something that offered the opportunity to strike out on one's own. The road was everything that the railway was not. It was, in the most fervent sense, a freeway.

By contrast, the early Canadian embrace of the highway was noticeably less enthusiastic. Viewed as something of a side venture, its main purpose was to capture the wallets of auto-addicted American citizens to the south. Beyond this, the government saw little need for highways, given that the country was well serviced by the train. That service included fresh whitefish caught at what is now the ghost town of Port Coldwell, Ontario, and served up for dinner in the dining car only minutes later. As often as not, the conductor could be counted on for a bottle of reasonably priced bootleg liquor. Parents thought little of sending an eight-year-old child on a train alone to go to school or to market. Some trains remained idle on the tracks while all aboard waited for a local woman's hen to lay eggs, so she could go further down the line to sell them.

That rather fabled component of the railway has become a thing of the past. Occasionally it receives sentimental or fetishistic lip service, but the train remains a mode of movement in drastic decline, and with good reason. In July 2007, ten out of twenty-six trains that set out from Winnipeg to Churchill, Manitoba, simply didn't arrive. Passenger trains setting out from anywhere else in Canada were chronically late, with the tardiness of Canadian trains increasing by sixty percent in 2007. Perhaps passengers have become annoyed by waiting on a siding while containers of anhydrous chlorine are green-lighted through, or perhaps it's those men in suits hovering around first class. Or the dining cars where, for twenty-five dollars, it is still possible to eat a perfectly good ten-dollar meal. For whatever reason, the train remains a method of travel studiously avoided by more than ninety percent of Canadian travellers.

Although efforts have been made to foist the familiar rhetoric of nation building that accompanied the railway onto the Trans-Canada Highway as well, they have been undertaken with considerably less conviction. Thus far, the highway hasn't received the full golden Last Spike treatment: it hasn't achieved the status of an unquestioned cultural icon or even a symbol that is mutually agreed upon. Nonetheless, progress is presumed of the highway, even demanded of it, and so is community.

It seems self-evident that the Trans-Canada Highway, a vast hard surface connecting St. John's, Newfoundland, with Tofino, British Columbia, would be a boon for the enrichment of friendship, family, community, and all the social aspects of the human tribe. That the road would bring Canadians closer together and knit them into a more integrated nationhood is presented as a long-established benefit of the Trans-Canada, but it is not a benefit that all communities necessarily want to share.

In November 1993, I arrived in a rented car at Tofino, on Vancouver Island, the final western stop of the Trans-Canada Highway. There I attached myself to the outskirts of a large gathering of knapsacked young people, all veterans of the road, all milling about, castaways in the rain telling eager stories of the vast clearcuts they had seen in their journeys. These were the new "long gone daddies" of the road, poets not so much of the environment as of environmental ruin. The tourist sites that formed the highlights of their journeys were not nature, but sites where nature had been mutilated. I stayed long enough to overhear a grim game of one-upmanship in which the young man who told the most graphic story about the most thoroughly destroyed piece of wilderness appeared to win the competition.

At the same time, the Tofino newspaper contained a story announcing that the town council had passed a resolution banning youth hostels. Although the road was in place that allowed young Canadians a chance to come to the perimeter of their country, there were some who didn't want them. They didn't want their cynicism, their environmental awareness, their nose rings, their incomprehensible lingo, and their empty wallets. They didn't want this makeshift "drifter tourism," as it has been called. What they wanted was mass tourism: families ensconced in vans and gas-hungry sports utility vehicles, tourists who would rent solid, overpriced motel rooms instead of kipping out for free in a tarp beneath the rain. What they were after was the officially stamped tourist who was committed to the road rituals of Edward McCourt and his wife or Mr. and Mrs. Nicholas Monsarrat, not penniless Jack Kerouacs and six-foot-tall, marijuana-smoking girlfriends who knew how to live on the bum.

Increasingly, the history of roadside accommodation shows a trend toward excluding the poorer traveller, with the banning of youth hostels just one glaring example. Another is the closing of free municipal campgrounds, which, ironically, were initiated in Canada by the Canadian Automobile Association in an attempt to stimulate car travel. In the U.S., these free sites began to disappear in the 1920s, at the same time as the car became an obtainable consumer good for the unwashed masses. Today, such campsites still exist along several Saskatchewan highways, complete with a cleared field, a tap, an outhouse, and perhaps a wooden box with a sign almost shyly asking for a donation. It's the sort of place where a small circus might set up, or a Roma camp. In some cases, the early days of taking to the road were known not only as "vagabonding," and "motor hoboing," but also "gypsying." All this was fine until actual "gypsies" themselves starting showing up, at which point the camps began to close down.

A former premier of Alberta, Ralph Klein, once famously arranged to give Alberta welfare recipients a free one-way bus ticket out of the province. His conception of the national high-way was as a road on which social problems ("Eastern creeps and bums," he called them) could be transported out of his province and into the maw of the big city where they properly belonged, and in a manner cheaper than could ever be done by the railway. The vision of a hundred busloads of impoverished Albertans convoying across the Prairies and then swooping down the Rocky Mountains into Vancouver, where they would all be handed a frothy moccachino, is certainly a vision of national unity, but it is also a measure of ignorance. The tensions between North and South, East and West, Small Town and Big City, are firmly entrenched in Canada, and while the Canadian road is often presented as a means of dismantling these prejudices, it also provides a formidable means of reinforcing them.

When the linking sections of the Trans-Canada were finally completed in the mid 1960s, connecting the small company and fishing towns of Lake Superior, residents there began for the first time to lock their doors, a defensive manoeuvre that had previously been unheard of. With the railroad representing the only way into town, all that was required to keep a town stranger-free was a police officer or a company security guard to wait at the station, where every stranger who stepped off the train would be told to get back on and keep moving. The road rendered this screening method impossible. Now, for the first time, some of the remote and insular towns of Canada were confronted with the phenomenon of the stranger, that lurking presence, a man whose name is not known, whose family is not known, and who has arrived for reasons that cannot be comprehended. Like it or not, the road was bulldozing a new vision of community onto the earth: an amorphous, kinetic, cosmopolitan community, born of the dangerous and erotic activities of the city, which thrived and depended on the stranger. From now on, unstable young men like the thinly fictionalized Dean Moriarity of *On the Road* could tuck his cigarette pack under the sleeve of his T-shirt, get behind the wheel of a car, and stay there for seventeen straight hours, emerging 1,180 miles later to turn his dangerous eyes on a twelve-year-old girl, steal your wallet, and throw up on your carpet. Community, home itself, had become subject to a new and threatening tempo.

Another of the great Canadian roads, the Alaska Highway, was built almost exclusively by strangers: American soldiers, forty per cent of them African-American, many of them, regardless of colour, unfamiliar with the cold. During the construction of this highway, officers found vehicles parked in the ditches, hardened soldiers sitting beside them, crying uncontrollably. Stalled vehicles were started by lighting a fire under the oil pan. Local radio communication was routinely blocked by the northern lights.

Just getting men in position to build this road required resourcefulness. One officer scoured local saw mills for all the sawdust he could find, which he then spread from bank to bank on the ice of a frozen river. Having preserved the ice for a while longer, he lay down a decking of heavy planks to spread the weight and sent his regiment across. In summer, certain sections of the road were so muddy that soldiers noticed that for every mile they drove, the odometer showed six miles; in other words, five miles of downward motion for each mile forward.

This massive road, some of which follows the routes explored by Charles Bedaux, brought forth the stranger in great numbers— and not only the stranger, but the black stranger. The officer in charge of the Alaskan Defense Command, Simon B. Buckner, believed that the vaunted communal aspect of road building was far from a good thing. In a letter to a fellow officer, he expressed concern that the highway would open up access to high-paying port jobs that would be taken by black soldiers working the highway

and cause them to . . . settle after the war, with the natural result that they would interbreed with the Indians and Eskimos and produce an astonishingly objectionable race of mongrels which would be a problem here from now on.

For all the vaunted freedom implied in the highway, the African-American experience of road has differed from the white experience. Where white writers and songsters have celebrated the highway as an opportunity for renewal and a chance to find their own freedom within vast spaces, African-American writers who took to the road in the mid-twentieth century typically drove at night, when they couldn't be seen, and resigned themselves to eating standing at "nigger windows" at restaurants. They also carried a copy of *Travelguide,* a black-oriented magazine that listed hotels and motels that might accept them. For them, the road was not a path toward renewal, personal freedom, and individuality; it was a sometimes dangerous reiteration of what they already knew. Today, there are initials that describe the difficulty and complexity of the road and its relationship to the "other": DWB (Driving while Black) and even WWB (Walking while Black). Being on the road as an African-American meant that, sooner or later, you could get flagged down by Jim Crow.

These days, the road as a meaningful cultural location has

taken on a definite rural flavour as a somewhat antiquated place having to do with identity and the old-fashioned rituals of finding oneself. In contemporary media discussion, the road has been largely replaced by the "street," a decidedly more urban location, and one in which African-American culture has not been excluded and in fact flourishes. While the street has engendered street fights, street people, street drugs, and street gangs, it has also given us street wisdom and street credibility, street parties, street sense, street music, such as rap and hip hop, and street culture. The street is youthful, hip, organic, and ever-changing. The street *is* home.

The road is where we go to find it.

8

VIRGIN TERRITORY

Highway 70, once known as Heenan's Highway after Ontario MPP Peter Heenan, is a 160-kilometre paved surface linking Kenora and Fort Frances. During the 1932 ceremony that opened this road, the premier of Ontario stood at the podium and observed that he had just driven through territory that Mr. Heenan had described as "virgin." Asked what exactly he meant by virgin territory, Mr. Heenan, standing next to him, answered, "Land where the hand of man had never set foot."

Unlike the official opening of the Trans-Canada three decades later, the rhetoric of nation building was absent from this ceremony. In its place was a hammy nod-and-wink vaudevillian performance that went over rather well. According to the premier, when they started out from Kenora he had been a good Presbyterian and Mr. Heenan a good Catholic. The weather, however, was so bad that by the time they reached Fort Frances, they were both Baptists.

The *Fort Frances Times* welcomed in the new road with an article written by the minister of highways. It is clear from this piece that, even as late as the 1930s, it was still not entirely clear to the Canadian public or its elected officials what exactly the new road was for. The province's chief road bureaucrat assumed from the start that the highway would be a major thoroughfare not only for vehicles but for *pedestrians* as well, an idea that today seems at best preposterous. The article is accompanied by an illustration of purposeful men in business suits marching about on a remote northern highway in the middle of the night while car traffic streams between them, casting precise and lifesaving cones of light.

The minister goes on to equate driving with Christian benevolence, in which the Golden Rule ought to prevail, particularly when it comes to safety. "We have all the advantage when we are driving," notes the minister, "let us not use that advantage in a bullying way." If drivers apply what he calls "the principles of COURTESY," he is confident that any nascent road rage can be nipped in the bud. At night, instructs the minister, it is crucial for the pedestrian to walk facing oncoming traffic and to carry some-

thing light for the beams of the oncoming cars to pick up. According to the minister, "a partly opened newspaper will do the trick." Perhaps the *Fort Frances Times*.

Heenan's Highway, like many of the existing roads of Canada, was a Depression era works project and testifies to the enormous, unsung, and largely undocumented role that the Depression work gang played in the building of the modern Canadian road. Those who drive the hundred or so miles of this highway will, in the blink of an eye, drive over the longest single-span wooden bridge in the world, a "timber trough truss bridge," the last remaining in Ontario. The road is immaculately maintained and finely graded and, like so many of the roads that cross the North, almost entirely free of traffic. It was built largely to stop the spread of disaffection and Bolshevism among unemployed Canadian workers who were often patrolled by police officers, while modern road-building equipment lay idle at the sides of the road.

‡

Just west of the southern terminus of Heenan's Highway is Fort Frances and the vast sprawl of Abitibi Consolidated, where several forests worth of spruce lie horizontally in the stacking yard. Among other things, beautifully designed novels are published on the paper that comes out of this mill. The smell in town is often gut-wrenching as a consequence of the kraft process that turns spruce trees into a viscous slough. To do this, the trees are hustled across a mill floor that runs the length of three football fields: an ungainly and unlikely operation that, when running smoothly, results in the production of 800 tons of paper a day. But even to notice the smell that clings to this town is to admit to a type of urban daintiness. "It's the smell of money," a resident tells me sharply. "So what if it stinks?" This honesty is echoed on a sign outside a local restaurant promising customers "Lousy food and warm beer."

The entrance to Fort Frances has been beautified by the La Verendrye Parkway, completed in 2003, a tailored lakeshore boulevard fitting snugly against the shores of the Rainy River and, I'm told, a vast improvement on the garbage, industrial debris, and mangled shopping carts that occupied the space previously. Minnesota sits on the other side, quiet, peaceful, as if unoccupied. Fort Frances, it turns out, is one of those delightful Canadian towns where it is possible to park your car on the main road and dive directly into the cold, bracing water. The picnic tables along the parkway have been thoughtfully supplied with empty tins of mashed potato mix to serve as ashtrays, and above the bike path, at evenly spaced intervals, hang idealized and dashing banner portraits of La Verendrye. He looks remarkably like Cyrano de Bergerac, carefree and ebullient, his face showing none of the heaviness you might expect of a man whose son was ritualistically decapitated by the Sioux in the course of a fur trade disagreement.

Highway 11 runs west out of Fort Frances through the tiny dots of Crozier, Devlin, Emo. Theoretically, this road is still part of Yonge Street in downtown Toronto, although how this connection is arrived at is not clear. And just to the south of this highway stands what the American traveller W.A. Kenyon called "the most spectacular prehistoric native monument in all of Canada," the largest burial mound site in the country.

These mounds, now located on the grounds of the Native-run Kay-Nah-Chi-Wah-Nung Historical Centre, represent the elaborate burial rituals of the Laurel culture, with generations of the deceased placed one on top of another. The burial mounds, encompassing at least 5,000 years of human activity, protrude from a flat prairie grass plain, silent and evocative. Behind them, the Rainy

River courses for a hundred miles, the original route that for centuries allowed the dead to be brought to this burial ground. According to a brochure, "The weight of history is on this place." That weight is inescapable: The quietude of a passed civilization emanates from those mounds, all of them covered in dense green grass and rising from the earth like the most organic of formations, looking both natural and human-made at the same time. The pelicans soar over top, immense charitable birds, circling in slow, narrowing gyres until they light without effort on the river.

Some thirty kilometres further west is the town of Rainy River. At one time, Rainy River was the hub of a different form of transportation: a divisional point for the CNR and port to innumerable ferry runs that set out to the freshwater sea known as Lake of the Woods. Rainy River is a town, like many towns, founded by trappers. It would seem that the highway has done little to bring the celebrated wealth of the south to this spot. In fact, the opposite appears to have taken place. A sign mounted on a building on the main street shouts, Rainy River: A Nice Place to Visit, a Better Place to Live. Every destitute stopping place is God's Country, and perhaps that's the way it should be. But there's something depressing about the optimism of this slogan. It feels as though the town itself has taken to the road and headed out somewhere else, leaving behind a number of buildings, including a towering Masonic lodge that now houses the library.

It is a reliable rule of the road that the health and vitality of any town can be accurately measured by the health and vitality of its local library. In Fort Frances, the children are streaming in and out, adults are seated at tables, and the computers are humming. In this one, there is barely a pulse. Two sullen teenage girls staff an otherwise empty room. The shelves are packed from floor to ceiling with shining oversized paperbacks featuring steamy paintings of gunslingers and breasty women on the covers. The effect is more like that of a bad secondhand bookstore on the verge of going out of business. The books are the sort that cottagers get rid of when they sell the cottage or head south in the fall—it's easier to dump them off at the library than to truck them to the landfill. Sunlight streams in through a large window in the library bathroom and, on a nail above the toilet, hangs a strategically placed flyswatter.

"All right," booms Deborah, clapping her hands together and pointedly addressing the two young girls at the front desk. "What is of historical interest in Rainy River?" She is prone to these outbursts of enthusiasm, but the two girls at the desk are only appalled by her. After a very long and uncomfortable silence, one of the girls, in a dubious whisper, says, "There's a museum in the train." Stunned by the boldness of her own claim, she immediately looks to her friend for confirmation. "Isn't there?"

Her companion is mortified to be drawn into such a discussion and answers coolly, even indignantly, "*I don't know!*"

"Well, there used to be," says the first girl.

"Yeah," says the other. "There used to be. I don't know if there is any more."

In fact, there is a museum by the train. I can see it out the window, fifty yards away. But the museum is closed, and, I find out later, will remain closed for a long time. The meagre funds required to pay a student to keep it open have not been found. Too bad. The weight of history lies heavily on this place. Funds have been found, however, to hire a student to staff a small modern office

next to the train, the tourist information office. To some extent, this is what the road has done: traded in history for tourism. The tall, earnest young man behind the desk explains that, yes, in fact the museum is closed, and should it ever open, it will not be open on Sunday, Monday, or Tuesday.

I unload a barrage of questions, and he at once drops the tourist board gimcrack and comes clean. "Nobody comes here," he says softly. "You're the first." The young people are getting out of here as fast as they can. "Calgary," he says. An almost mystical light shines in his face. Calgary.

Next door stands the prominently mounted street sign that announces Yonge Street. In front of it is the official blue information sign, pleased to explain that Rainy River is connected by this road to the humming frenzy of Toronto, 1,915 kilometres away. This, then, is Main Street: main street Rainy River, main street Toronto— what Sinclair Lewis, in his novel of the same name, sneeringly calls "the climax of civilization." Smart-alecky, quick-talking VJs are forever zipping up here to film this sign for television programs that will be called "Road Trip" or "On the Road." And yet Toronto exerts no pull here. In this hidden corner of Ontario, sometimes called the Northwest Angle, the tug is tangibly westward. The roads lead there, the rivers lead there, the culture leads there, the fur trappers went there before us, breaking the routes that the highways would follow. The young people are going there too. They follow the road. West.

It is obvious that the young man is itching to quit this job and go there himself. He staffs a room packed to overflowing with tourist brochures that have officially branded Rainy River, somewhat unfortunately, as "Sunset Country." There are more brochures here than there are residents in town. "There's the bison farm," he says, rousing himself from his dreams of westward realization. But he can no longer summon the enthusiasm and his voice is flat and unconvincing. In the brochure, even the bison look small and underfed. They seem to understand that their fate is to be sent down a number of paved highways in the hope that someone will pay money to eat them, more money than a hamburger, more even than the Trans-Canada twelve-inch hotdog. Despite the brochures, the future does not seem to be in bison burgers.

These antiseptic and portable rooms go by the name Tourist Resource Centre or some such dizzying variant, and they represent the cultural roadkill of the highway. Knocked senseless in a collision between how the road was envisioned and how it actually played out, these curious institutions have managed to drag themselves off the highway to set up here on the side. They stand in the belief that the "Highways of Hope" will finally deliver that great payload of tourist money, preferably in U.S. currency, and that all is good, good, and better.

At the same time, these slogans also teem with contempt for the actual tourist. It is there in the unquestioned assumption, insistence even, that the tourist is positively laden with money and eager to hand it over for a hunk of cooked buffalo meat. It is there in the audacity of the claims made: that Rainy River, despite being the physical dead end of Highway 11, is the "Gateway to Northwestern Ontario." It is there in that dreadful unyielding optimism that invites people to come to a place that "offers unparalleled opportunities as a vacation destination"—opportunities that include "free public access to the river," "birdwatching," and a trip to the railway museum, even though the museum is closed and, it seems, always will be.

Outside the museum stands Steam Engine 4008, a "Santa Fe" type steam engine
"donated" to the town nearly half a century ago and now the centre piece of the
Heritage Square History Museum. Despite
the road's having long turned this massive piece of technology into a fossil, it
has been lovingly maintained, with an elaborate, painstakingly
hand-painted sign that, with its faint bitterness and the mind-bog-
gling labour put into it, is more revealing than the engine itself.
Also included in "the museum," is a comprehensive "free" hand-
out that lists everything from "haulage rating" (sixty-five per cent)
to locomotive class (T-la).

The trains, of course, do not stop here, and they haven't for
years. What is on display here is not history or heritage but a fas-
cination with big machines and a longing for the days when we
were young and gainfully employed, and massive engines obeyed
our will and our touch. The road has continued on, and the great
symbols of our coal-burning youth are now maintained by aging
men who write longingly of the old days.

A short distance away, on Highway 11, a quiet vehicular rustle
intermittently continues alongside the ancient burial mounds of
Kay-Nah-Chi-Wah-Nung. The 4008 is gone, and so are the "hay
lanterns," the "blow-off cocks," the "counter-balance wheels," and
the "steam injector." Motion has changed, and the language of
motion has changed with it. The pedal is now pressed firmly to
the metal.

I HOPE SUCH A THING WILL NEVER HAPPEN AGAIN.
—PERCY MORRISON, CORONER, 1896

CAR-NAGE

The world's first fatal automobile accident took place on August 31, 1869, when Mary Ward, of Dublin, Ireland, was thrown from a steam-powered vehicle and crushed beneath one of its wheels. An astronomer, artist, scientist, author, mother of five, and one of three women in the world to be on the mailing list of the Royal Astronomical Society—Queen Victoria was another—she was also the first person to write, illustrate, and publish a book about the microscope, on which she was an expert. *Sketches with a Microscope* was reprinted eight times in her lifetime.

After her death, a local newspaper reported that "the utmost gloom pervaded the town." This gloom was compounded by the shocking novelty of the death and the gruesome defeat the human body suffers in a contest against an automobile. A coroner's inquest concluded that the victim's neck and jaw bone had been broken, that she had been bleeding profusely from her mouth, nose, and ears, and that after going into violent spasms, she was dead within three minutes. "I felt a slight jolt," said one of the passengers, referring to the wheels going over her body—perhaps the first time this eerie and too familiar phrase had found such usage. The car, as in many early fatalities, was travelling between three and four miles an hour, about the speed of a brisk walk, and no blame was attached to the accident.

Twenty-seven years later, Bridget Driscoll, on her way to a folk dancing exhibition on the grounds of the Crystal Palace in London, England, became the world's second known automobile fatality when she was struck and killed by a car belonging to the Anglo-French Motor Carriage Company, which was giving free demonstration rides to the public. The car was gasoline-powered, making Bridget Driscoll the world's first recorded petrol vehicle fatality. In this case as well, the driver claimed to have been travelling at about four miles per hour, although witnesses insisted he was going up to three times that speed. It was also said that the driver was deeply engrossed in conversation with his passenger, a young woman, perhaps the first appearance of the courtship rituals that are now embedded in car culture and account for no end of dubious driving. Again the coroner assigned no blame and uttered what today sounds like the most astonishing of statements: "I hope," he said, "such a thing will never happen again." Today, Mrs. Driscoll's fatal encounter on the road is often used as the starting date for measuring the world's traffic fatalities.

In North America, the first road death caused by an automobile took place in New York in 1899, when Henry Hale Bliss stopped to help a woman disembark from a streetcar near Central Park and was fatally wounded by an electric-powered taxi cab that crushed his head and chest. The cabbie was charged with manslaughter and acquitted. In Canada, there seems to be no formal record of our first automobile fatality, although seven years after the death of Henry Hale Bliss, a bizarre Canadian connection was provided when the prominent American scientist, explorer, meteorite collector, and museum builder, Henry Augustus Ward, was killed in a car accident.

The death of Henry Ward—presumably no relation to Mary Ward—brought to an end the long and distinguished career of one of the world's great collectors of geological specimens. In 1858, Ward sailed the West African coast to Lagos, where he undertook a hundred-mile walk to the interior city of Abeokuta and witnessed the military review of a division of Amazons. He also studied the source of the mysterious musical sands of Gebel-Nakous. On the heels of these adventures, a concerned aunt wrote to him about his pursuits, "I am beginning to think that nothing less striking than being eaten up by cannibals or falling into the crater of a volcano will suffice you for a finale of your adventures." In fact, Henry Ward's finale was, by today's standards, a much more mundane affair. On a summer afternoon in 1906, he stepped off a Chicago street corner and was struck and killed by an oncoming car. Ward had ignored the brave motto that prefaced his earliest journal, written as a schoolboy in Wyoming: "Be right and then go ahead."

Aside from visiting Canada to collect meteorites, Henry Ward had previously made a brief trip to Southern Ontario following the strange events of September 15, 1885. On that day, a Northern Trunk freight train, driven at high speeds by engineer William

Burnip, crossed Arthur Street in downtown St. Thomas, Ontario, and struck and killed the one creature, with the exception of Mickey Mouse, to have had its name canonized in dictionaries of the English language—Jumbo the elephant, the backbone of P.T. Barnum's Greatest Show on Earth, a show that also included an early American automobile among its curiosities.

Ward, who was in written contact with many of the great scientists of his day, was also a colleague, friend, and correspondent of P.T. Barnum. Two years before Jumbo was struck dead in St. Thomas, Barnum had written Ward granting him complete authority to deal with Jumbo's remains in the case of the animal's demise and urging him "to lose no time in saving his skin & skeleton."

Until Jumbo was struck dead, the town of St. Thomas was principally known from a brief mention in Anna Jameson's *Winter Rambles and Summer Studies in Canada*. In that book, published in 1839, she ascribes to the town "three churches, one of which is very neat; and three taverns." It was also, at the time of Jumbo's arrival, the site of Canada's largest lunatic asylum. On the day after the accident, two hundred men armed with rope and tackle managed to topple the eight-ton carcass down the embankment and clear the busy tracks.

By the time Ward arrived, the residents of St. Thomas were already emulating the hucksterism of Jumbo's famous owner. Enterprising locals charged five cents admission to see Jumbo's

carcass. Slivers were chipped off the tusks and sold, until a patrolling constable put a stop to the practice. Under Ward's command, six local butchers were hired to cut up the meat. The viscera were burnt, and as the smell of broiled elephant wafted through St. Thomas, the *Daily Times* began selling its hastily printed Jumbo Memorial Tablets:

JUMBO
King of Elephants,
Died at ST. THOMAS, Sept. 15, 1885,
AGED 24 YEARS
The pillar of a people's hope,
The centre of the world's desire.

All that remained of Jumbo was a flood of elephant grease, bottled and sold as a curative ointment for aches and pains.

The death of Jumbo spawned an industry of relics and memorabilia, and left in its wake one of the more noticeable "roadside attractions": the life-sized Jumbo that currently overlooks the highway leading into town, commissioned by the St. Thomas town council on the centenary of Jumbo's death. The engineers who designed the road had not anticipated that a full-scale sculpture of the world's largest elephant would one day have to pass under the bridges of the Trans-Canada Highway. As a result, the sculpture underwent the indignity of having its legs cut off and reattached in St. Thomas, Ontario.

=|=

Since 1896, when Bridgett Driscoll met her death on her way to a folk dancing exhibition, an estimated thirty million people have been killed on the world's roads. Many millions more have been injured, and every year sees a further 1.2 million killed and ten times that number seriously hurt. In Canada, the numbers are no less grim. Every day, six hundred Canadians are involved in road accidents. A man, woman, or child is injured on the road every seven minutes, and every three hours one of us is killed.

This does not stop us from taking to the road in vast numbers, nor does it concern us enough to compel us back onto the horse, or even the train, neither of which is risk-free. In 1867, in New York City, four pedestrians a week were getting killed by horses. In Canada, in the first year of the transcontinental rail line, astonishing numbers of people were run down and killed while walking on the tracks.

A great many of these deaths have been attributed to an epic national fondness for alcohol. This would tally with contemporary research showing that today nearly half the people who are struck and killed by a vehicle while *walking* are themselves intoxicated. On the road, even drinking and walking don't mix. For the most part, the anti-drunk-driving movement has fixed blame on the drinking driver and downplayed the fact that drunk drivers primarily kill themselves, followed by their passengers, who are usually intoxicated as well. Drunken pedestrians—and drunken cyclists—also fall victim at high rates to drivers, both drunk and sober. The complicity of victim and perpetrator, in terms of their alcohol consumption, does nothing to reduce the tragedy, but it does indicate that a solution is not a simple black and white morality play in which the drinking driver is demonized. It is generally maintained that the lives saved by effective anti-drunk-driving strategies will be, for the most part, the lives of the drunk drivers themselves. In the United States, where the right to drive has been called more important than the right to vote, the combination of drinking and driving is set so deep into social institutions that U.S. experts consider the elimination of drinking and driving to be an unrealistic goal. On both sides of the border, the recognition of just how many drinking drivers take to the road at any given moment has compelled some traffic safety experts to suggest that a special dedicated lane be set aside, reserved exclusively for drivers who have been drinking.

The road has always been an establishment that caters to the alcohol-inclined. As a retail point for alcoholic beverages, it is extremely well stocked. There are gas stations that sell alcohol. There are drive-up windows that sell alcohol. And there is, of course, the roadhouse, an institution that couldn't exist without a cozy relationship between booze and the highway. Such premises are legally required to provide parking spaces to the people who drive up to drink there. The car itself is often the first and preferred drinking location of young people.

All these inducements to drink and then drive are countered by a public and much-repeated message that insists drinking and driving are entirely incompatible. Acronyms such as MADD, SADD, and PRIDE have become commonplace, and their workers and founders are honoured by governments even as those governments work harder and harder to extend drinking hours and increase the availability of alcohol. But whatever isn't yet known about the drinking and driving problem, there is one thing that is known for certain: increasing punishment for the drunk driver doesn't work, has never worked, and apparently never will work. What works is swift court arraignments and swift sentencing; reducing the number of cars on the road, especially those driven by sixteen-year-olds; and some form of limited prohibition on the sale of alcohol. A vast body of research shows that any brewery that offers a reduced rate on its product, then closes its ads by urging its customers to drive safely and drink responsibly, is engaging in a strategy it knows will not work. Similarly, the policymakers behind federal legislation to toughen Canadian drinking and driving laws are aware in advance that such policies will be ineffective. They also know that focusing blame and anger on the drinking driver will generate slavish media coverage and is significantly cheaper than hiring more judges to facilitate swift court trials.

The face of this hypocrisy is neatly revealed in the T-shirt that states, "Don't Drink and Drive. You Might Hit a Bump and Spill Your Drink." The slogan sounds the difficulty of confronting the "alcohol crash" problem in a country that, like many northern countries, has traditionally possessed an extremely robust appetite for booze. Early Canadian travellers reported that on pioneer roads leading into Prairie towns, the alarming din of drunken revellers was audible long before the town itself could even be seen. From the sailor to the voyageur to the hardened crew that followed Alexander Mackenzie onto the Bella Coolla River, Canadian travel was for centuries dependent on the regular consumption of alcohol. To not provide stiff drinks to the men who did the hard work of transporting goods across Canada was unthinkable. Moving from that paradigm to one in which the driver is expected to be absolutely sober has proved a difficult national exercise, and one that today results in some 1,500 alcohol-related road deaths a year. It is particularly difficult in places like Nova Scotia, where public transportation is almost nonexistent and road crashes kill about one young person per week—well below the national average, but a rate devastating to a small province.

In the early days of automotive travel, the flask was considered, like a map, a pair of goggles, or leather gauntlets, an essential piece of motoring gear. When Dr. Doolittle, fresh from his cross-Canada road trip, stood up before the Empire Club in 1925, he had no qualms about launching into a series of jocularly intimate drinking jokes: "I would just like to say to the bootleggers in the audience that there is a man [the Maine water bottler, Hiram Ricker] that has made millions out of the finest booze that God ever put into the granite rocks of the state of Maine. There is not a headache in a gallon." Today, it is impossible to imagine a road or motoring official who would position alcohol and road use in the same sentence and try to get a laugh out it.

Wilby himself was a dedicated friend of the flask, and it wasn't just him who began a road trip with a great snort of something. In the late 1940s, French author Simone de Beauvior thought nothing of motoring across America sloshed on martinis. Luckily, she seems to have done no more damage than write a book about the experience.

The well-known phrase "one for the road" underscores just how closely having a drink and taking to the road are equated. One of its earliest citations is in *The Times* of March 1939: "Propaganda should be employed to train and fortify public opinion in the condemnation of persons who drink before driving—above all to discourage the practice of 'one for the road.'" Those quotation marks indicate that the term had been around for some time. The phrase took popular hold when Johnny Mercer used it in the lyrics of his song "One for My Baby (and One More for the Road)," which he wrote in 1943:

We're drinking my friend
To the end of a brief episode

So make it one for my baby
And one more for the road

Today, the phrase has earned its own rebuttal slogan: "None
for the Road."

Strange as it sounds now, the connection between alcohol consumption and road carnage wasn't self-evident. The first appearance of a drinking and driving fatality in American literature
occurs in *The Great Gatsby*. There, the highball-sodden Daisy
Buchanan, driving Gatsby's Rolls-Royce, accidentally runs down
her husband's mistress. Daisy has spent the afternoon drinking
cocktails in a stifling New York hotel room, and the dead woman's
husband, a gas station owner, George Wilson, who wrongly be-
lieves Gatsby was driving, expresses what is the response of many
people who have lost a loved one to a drunk driver:

"He murdered her."
"It was an accident, George."
Wilson shook his head.

In Canada, impaired drivers account for roughly half of highway fatalities, killing themselves and others at the rate of four people a day. But accounts of this carnage—whether the result of
drunk or sober activities—rarely make their way into the popular
depictions of the road, where the highway is presented as a passage
to freedom, fulfillment, and non-stop shopping.

=⊨

The highway is also very much a place where we die or suffer serious injury. We take to the road like young soldiers in search of adventure, confident that it will always be the other guy who gets it. In fact, over the course of our lives, nearly every Canadian (ninety-five per cent) will be involved in a road accident. When Prime Minister John Diefenbaker offered his hope that the new Trans-Canada Highway would "never hear the marching of warlike feet," he was ignoring the fact that Canadian roads, *prior* to the opening of the Trans-Canada, killed and wounded, yearly, more than twice the number of Canadian soldiers killed or wounded, yearly, during the Second World War. In the five years following the war, 205,000 Canadians were killed or injured in traffic accidents, and the numbers were increasing sharply. If, in 1949, Canadian taxpayers had been told that their highway system was incurring casualties at a rate that dwarfed the death toll of World War II, it is doubtful the government would have received the green light to proceed with the construction of the Trans-Canada—a road guaranteed to significantly increase those casualties.

Just keeping up with the numbers of people killed and wounded on the road requires extensive labyrinths of bureaucracy. These include a tax-supported network of names ranging from Transport Canada to the Fatality Database to the Serious Injury Database, both operated by TIRF, the Traffic Injury Research Foundation, which is not to be confused with CCMTA, the Canadian Council of Motor Transport Administrators. All of these organizations, along with others, share the task of sifting through the traffic accident numbers and employing a bewildering variety of "data capture procedures" in an attempt to make sense of them. This is a far cry from a 1930s Ontario transport minister's suggestion that pedestrians protect themselves on the highway by holding a folded newspaper in front of them.

Little did the minister know, for example, that the road system of Canada would soon be requiring five million tons of road salt each winter, or that this salt would attract large animals to the sides of roads, and that those animals would in turn increase the death rates among drivers. Road salt is scattered on the roads of the nation and works by breaking the bond between snow and pavement, creating a layer of brine that has a freezing point of less than zero degrees. With an estimated 1.4 million kilometres of roads in Canada, this means that each kilometer of Canadian road receives approximately three and a half tons of salt each year. These numbers don't apply to regions of the country that frequently have winter temperatures below the freezing point of brine.

Although ice is typically a hazard of the winter road, it is on some occasions the road itself. Ice roads, a Canadian invention, are thoroughfares built on frozen lakes and rivers or on frozen ground and are meant to last from freeze-up to early March. Such roads serve remote Native communities and connect places such as Wawakapewin and Kasobonika, Ogoki and Nakina, or Sachigo Lake and Keewaywin. These are true folk roads, like winding winter sentences writ in a Native language, and they require folk strategies to drive them. In spring, when the ice is on the verge of breaking up, these roads are driven with one hand on the wheel

and the other on the door handle. Such roads are considered no longer functional once the first vehicle goes through, and bets are sometimes laid as to whose it will be.

Northern ice roads were pioneered by an ex-Mountie, John Denison, who was awarded the Order of Canada for his work, and they extend beyond the tree line into the Arctic. Some of the these roads are nearly a thousand kilometres long, such as the ice highway connecting Yellowknife to the Tahera Diamond Corporation's Jericho mine.

For two months every winter, trucks passed over this ice highway twenty-four hours a day, seven days a week, in convoys of two to five, on ice five to six feet thick. Truckers have likened the surface to "floating pavement," and in fact the road is not slippery and smooth but washboard rough, with pressure cracks, ice ripples, and fissures along the length of it. Ice roads are notoriously tricky. In John Denison's opinion, "The only fellow who knows anything about ice is in his first or second year working on it, because he still has some confidence left. The longer you stay with it, the less you know."

Travel on these roads is slow to avoid something called a popout, where the weight and speed of the vehicle pushing down on the ice force a wave of water to roll forward beneath the ice. Drivers, when approaching land or meeting oncoming trucks, reduce speed even further to prevent an "ice wave rebound." There are also the problems of "ground drifting." Ice truckers are presumably brave men, but there is one thing at least that they publicly admit to be being afraid of: warm weather.

Such roads are Northern incarnations of Charles Bedaux's highway through the mountains—dangerous, improbable, temporary thoroughfares that go as far as the road can possibly take us. These roads have also allowed Canada to become the world's third-largest producer of diamonds and are undertaken by fully loaded sixty-two-ton B-trains or ninety-ton heavy haulers on "hook-and-drop trips." Journeys on these pathways involve an unremitting sameness of vast boreal or treeless flats, interrupted by the sighting of a wolverine, or, as one driver noted, an upside-down rainbow, which he attributed to the ice crystals in the air. Global warming, however, may soon spell the end of the ice road altogether. In 2006, for the first time in the trucking industry's history, the ice didn't freeze up to the required minimum depth of forty inches (102 centimetres).

At one time, the truck driver represented a romantic appeal to adventure and innocence as a sort of modern cowboy who rode the wide open spaces of North America, singing the song of individualism and freedom while painfully missing his wife back home. In Canada, the trucker occupied an idealized space vacated by the voyageur a century earlier, and for a time the trucker was widely considered the most courteous and intelligent driver on the road. Before the insurance people got involved, they could also be counted on to pick you up when you were hitchhiking.

Today, that interpretation of the trucker is a thing of the past. Long-distance hauling is now subjected to Charles Bedaux–like speed-up systems to increase profit and has turned the modern trucker into a time–distance facilitator who is often forced to rely on little white pills, poor judgment, and speeding to get to his destination on time.

During the summer of 2004, driving between Wawa and Chapleau on Highway 101, I witnessed an encounter between two eastbound trucks that resembled a full-scale battle of dinosaurs. Whatever loyalty truckers feel toward one another, it was decidedly not on display here as one massive rig tried desperately to pass the other, only to be deliberately and repeatedly cut off. The dogfight went on for twenty miles, at which point one of the trucks, lagging visibly, gave up the fight with a furious bellow of his horn, tauntingly returned by the lead truck.

Such antagonisms are perhaps inevitable in a working environment where the hours are, to say the least, long. In Canada, the Ontario Trucking Authority has recently begun to petition the transportation ministry to reduce working hours by twenty-five per cent, a good idea given that nearly half the trucks pulled over on Canadian roads prove to be faulty (some have been found with their transmission held in place by a piece of string). It is not surprising that, these days, books about the trucking business bear titles like *Sweatshop on Wheels*. The romance of long-distance hauling has been further damaged by studies showing that, in some countries, the trucker is a leading vector in the spread of AIDS.

For the most part, trucks stick to main highways, with about two per cent of the road network handling about forty per cent of all truck activity. An average kilometre of main highway in Ontario bears some 2,300 trucks a day, although main expressways such as Highway 401 may experience a volume exceeding 10,000 trucks a day, while highways around Toronto routinely handle 40,000 trucks a day. This is non-stop cargo traffic with every imaginable freight pouring into the city, including runaway children transported back to their foster homes by exhausted CAS workers and incarcerated criminals who are routinely transported back and forth for the simple reason that there aren't enough cells to contain them—the road now acting as a permanent moving prison. In this vast, moving market, there are flatbed trucks filled with honey bees that will be rented out to farmers to pollinate their crops and goods purchased on what used to be called the information superhighway and downloaded onto the paved one. Morels, chanterelles, and matsutake mushrooms, packed in Styrofoam boxes and cooled with blue gel packs, are truck-bound to Vancouver airport and flown to Tokyo, where they'll sell for $150 per pound. Every day, 140 trucks are required to take the packaging these goods come in out of Toronto to U.S. landfills.

For all the cost-cutting, the caffeine pills, and the eighteen-wheel rigs held together by duct tape, truckers are in fact less likely to be involved in accidents than the rest of us. But they play a disproportionate role in the problem of road carnage: four per cent of road accidents, but eleven per cent of the fatalities. For the most part, these accidents occur during broad daylight on dry roads during clear weather. Eighty per cent of the time, it isn't the trucker but the driver or occupants of the other vehicle who are killed. About ten per cent of the time, it's a pedestrian.

In the modern hauling environment, where the size of the rig can force a trucker to drive a hundred miles to find a place to stop or turn around, it's not uncommon for truckers to pee in a bottle. Once filled, these bottles are often chucked out the windows, where, depending on state or provincial legislation, they may be regarded as hazardous waste. Trucker bombs, as they're called, are particularly annoying to roadside cleanup crews. The bottles, usually plastic beverage containers bought from convenience stores, are typically capped, and generally keep their seal even after being tossed from a moving vehicle. In the full glare of summer heat, pressure builds up inside and the "bombs," if nudged by a scythe or lawnmower or errant work boot, often explode. Department of Transportation road crews in the state of Utah alone pick up 20,000 such bottles a year. In the state of Wyoming, a trucker who heaves his pee bottle out the window of his cab faces a nine-month jail sentence.

Truck driver forums universally condemn the practice, and according to roadsideamerica.com, truckers themselves have perhaps been unfairly "stained" by the accusations. There is at least one incident on record, however, in which a rig driver was found dead in a one-vehicle accident in the state of Utah with his trousers down and an open plastic bottle on the floor of the cab. Publicly, truckers themselves have little tolerance for colleagues who engage in this practice, and one trucker who maintains a website glossary of trucking terms officially defines a trucker who hurls a pee bottle out the window as "Asshole Number 2," placing him between "Asshole Number 1: A bad or inconsiderate driver" and "Asshole Number 3: A driver who throws his litter bag out the window."

U.S. road authorities have lately become concerned about pee bottle "crossover," a phenomenon that sees the larger road-using population jettisoning pee bottles. Over the length of a hundred-mile stretch in Washington State, road crews cleaned up more than a thousand pee bottles in a single month, suggesting it isn't just truckers who are in too much of a hurry to stop and relieve themselves. In Canada, provincial road crews obligingly clean them up at taxpayers' expense and take

them to what *highwaySTAR* magazine calls "a suitable disposable site." Perhaps they mean a toilet.

⊐⊢

Barely visible on a tract of mowed grass on the Queen Elizabeth Way sits a plastic floral wreath, supported by a white stick that may or may not represent a cross. I pass it frequently and am always struck by the audacity of it: the sheer audacity that says that any human life, even one coursing by at 120 kilometres an hour on a sixteen-lane highway, is worthy of commemoration. Traffic roars alongside it, a continuous obliterating din that deafens even our belief in the healing capacity of silence, and yet this symbol stands, futile, beautiful, and brave at the same time. As roadside graffiti, it recalls an outrageously elaborate piece of work painted on a railway bridge above Queen Street a half mile away. There, someone took his—or her—life in his hands to dangle from a busy train bridge and pay tribute to his own creative impulse: the human urge to apply colour to a blank space.

Similarly, to erect this anonymous roadside monument on the QEW, a man or woman took extraordinary risks. To park here on the shoulder at any time of the day or night appears obviously suicidal, and yet to come the other way, from the land, so to speak, involves scaling a formidable fence and crossing two sets of daunting and heavily used train lines. Yet there it stands, anonymous, defiant, and barely visible.

Such roadside monuments, often with crosses, flowers, and photographs, are thought to have originated in the Southwestern United States from old Catholic traditions inherited from Spain and Mexico. They differ from customary death and burial rituals in that they occur outside of the graveyard and are planted defiantly in places where they can't help but be seen. And the people who see them are almost exclusively those who take to the road. For that brief moment in which they flit by the windshield, those informal crosses and floral arrangements pay a swift, anonymous tribute to the dead and, unlike other burial practices, enshrine and mark the actual location where death occurred.

The emergence of such symbols is so recent as to have escaped statistical scrutiny. A survey undertaken by the Maryland Department of Transportation estimated that road memorials, or "markers," are erected following ten to twenty per cent of fatal crashes. Such numbers have caused concern for local governments in both the U.S and Canada, so much so that the Alberta Department of Infrastructure and Transportation states that the erection of roadside memorials "is strongly discouraged," on the grounds that they represent a serious roadside safety hazard, either by distracting the driver of a vehicle or by being run into by errant vehicles that have left the road.

Furthermore, people are now getting killed or injured *while attending* or paying tribute to roadside memorials. In June of 2006, two teenage girls suffered serious injury when they were struck by a vehicle while visiting a roadside memorial outside of Sudbury, Ontario. Public reaction was far from sympathetic. Some letter writers urged that the people who erected this roadside memorial should be charged themselves. Others wanted the injured girls to have their licences suspended "for being stupid enough to park, at that hour, in the dark." The same letter writer suggested that the life-threatening injuries suffered by the teenagers were an example of "natural selection," an opinion the *Northern Life* newspaper didn't hesitate to publish. By doing so, they brought forth a new and startling vision of the road as a public space where the less bright among us go to be exterminated in the name of intellectually purifying the nation.

Governments both here and south of the border have been caught off guard by the phenomenon of the roadside monument and the intensity of feelings it evokes. The official interpretation, that such monuments are a distraction to drivers and therefore a safety threat, is significantly different from the public's concern. In 2004, highway officials in the state of Nevada removed an eight-foot tall steel cross from a Highway 50 right-of-way after a citizen threatened a lawsuit for allowing a religious symbol to be placed on public land. The cross was meant to mark the death, not of a highway casualty but a murder victim, a child. Suddenly, the highway was being used to commemorate not only its own victims, but the victims of all forms of violent death.

For the most part, we prefer death on the road to remain mute, contained, and beyond the reach of politics. Yet these monuments offer an unsanctioned and subversive form of *samizdat*. They insist that, despite the teeming monolithic anonymity of the busy modern road, the person whom we love demands to be honoured just as much as the young men and women whose lives end in a roadside explosion in Afghanistan, whose returning remains are often marked by Highway of Heroes ceremonies in which the Canadian flag is draped from an overpass. These roadside monuments, on the other hand, are the yellow ribbons in the private war that the road wages against us, stating in their own way, "Support Our Troops." They insist that a human life matters, even if the victims don't carry a gun and no vested interest rises up to support them or decry their deaths, or to call them heroes.

Although these monuments may contain names and dates painted on their surface, they remain, to the vast majority of road users, startling in their anonymity. They represent a folk expression, independent of the state or any formal instruction on how we are to grieve. As such, they have incurred the wrath of the state. In fairness, it is not a blind or totalitarian wrath but a considered and plodding one—one that remains a step behind the pace of the road and the ever-changing demands that the road makes upon us.

What road authorities invariably object to is that these monuments are *not the same*. They differ in size, in location, in materials used, flying in the face of the engineering conformity that the road has traditionally exalted in. They also disturbingly link the road not to freedom and progress but to blind and meaningless death. Their effect is to produce discomfort, expressed in the very language that road authorities employ to deal with them. According to a brief by the Alberta Department of Infrastructure and Transportation, "When a roadside memorial poses a hazard to the travelling public a district representative will contact the person who placed the display if his or her identity is known, and negotiate relocation to the fence line."

"Negotiate relocation to the fence line" is a bald and bureaucratic attempt to bury grief beneath almost militaristic jargon. It is a phrase that abjectly denies what is occurring on the road. Even the insistence that roadside monuments "pose a hazard to the travelling public" is a disingenuous attempt to redirect the blame for road carnage from the people who build, manage, and use the road to the people who put up a monument to someone who has perished on it.

While highway officials may remain trapped in a language that denies the reality of the road, they're not heartless, and efforts are underway to decently sort out the confusions. Typically, roadside monuments are dealt with by the bureaucratic turning of a blind eye. In Canada, local road authorities regularly allow a grace period of several months before removing the memorials. The impulse toward standardization is strong, with Alberta encouraging the grieving friends and relatives of road victims to enroll in its Adopt a Highway Program. Under this scheme, the province displays an "In memory of . . ." tab on a Caring for Alberta Highways sign. Many jurisdictions in the U.S. are opting for similar approaches. Such memorializing may lack the personal intensity and sheer dramatics of a roadside cross and floral arrangement, but they do appease the bureaucratic demand for road uniformity.

Waiting with open arms to help meet this demand is the private sector, with such companies as roadsidememorials.com offering standardized three-foot by twenty-inch "solid oak crosses stained and tipped with gold corners and complimented with a flower arrangement and a picture cover." These weather-resistant crosses are available for $100 US (personalized engraving, $50 US extra). Potential purchasers are reminded that "roadsidememorial.com will not be responsible for any accidents or injuries due to the placement of your cross," and that, furthermore, crosses placed on the sides of public roads may be removed "by authorities."

Despite occasional protestations, public hand-wringing, and the dedication of World Health Day 2004 to the theme of road safety, death on the road has been accepted as the inevitable price of taking to it. The modern road *is* a killing ground, far more deadly, numerically, than the modern battlefield, and it is accepted as such. To some extent, we even embrace it. High-velocity vehicular impact is now an industry onto itself. Sexualized and fetishized in books and movies, it has long been a staple of the North American film industry, predating even Charles Bedaux's madcap scheme to film his exploding Citroëns high up in the Rocky Mountains. Recently, an Andy Warhol painting of a crashed car, the iconic *Green Car Crash (Green Burning Car 1)*, sold for nearly $72 million. Websites such as wreckedexotics.com encourage viewers to send in their accident photos and stories. They insist, rather unconvincingly, that these countless full-colour displays will serve as a warning to other motorists. For whatever reason, these warnings are backed up by advertisements featuring girls in G-strings. Like any fetish, crashes have their own intimate and exclusionary lingo. Motorcyclists don't allow themselves to merely get into an accident. Instead, they "lay the bike down," as one might a bride on her wedding night.

The road has long been a dangerous place: from the falling trees that threatened Iroquois travellers to falling hydro wires, the opportunities for sudden death or trauma are many and varied. In taking to the road, we engage in a multiplicity of dangerous activities, including what is perhaps the most dangerous activity of all: we attempt to leave home, or to find it. We also try to change ourselves, to engage in a personal rebellion, to recover from a painful breakup, or to escape the most determined stalker of them all, ourselves. It is on the road that we paradoxically attempt to satisfy two fundamental needs: the urge to be alone and the urge for community. All of this activity is fraught with danger, which the young Lieutenant Le Couteur paid tribute to when he swooned over a teenage girl for putting a boat hook in a bear's eye to get where she was going.

 Mario Buda, a militant anarchist, attested to this struggle on September 16, 1920, when he used the corner of Wall Street to detonate a bomb from a horse-drawn carriage. The incident demonstrated the vulnerable intimacy created by the urban road and the way it meanders into the heart of the city, into the community, and into the family. His hatred for all these things lay beyond even the road's ability to heal him. Buda brought rage and terror to the streets of North America. In exploding a prototype of the world's first car bomb, Buda brought to full realization the early possibility of the vehicle as a projectile and the road as a means of conducting war. Since Buda's time, the road has changed from a method of taking armies *into* battle and become the battleground itself.

Even without the death tolls exacted by improvised roadside explosives and the Mario Buda types, we are swept away on the road in numbers that are almost too large to imagine: more than fifty million wounded worldwide each year, and more than a million killed. The numbers themselves are numbing, almost inconceivable, and seem, perversely, to throw a safety net around us as individual road users, as if such mass devastation somehow ensures that it could never happen to us. Culturally, without even thinking about it, we have accepted this carnage as the price of taking to the road. We have made a pact. We drive vehicles that their makers boldly call Fury or Mustang, LeSabre or Cutlass. Sometimes, in a bizarre bit of appropriation, a line of vehicles is named after a legendary Native American warrior, such as Chief

Pontiac. One can only wonder what the Chrysler Company had in mind when it named one of its cars De Soto, after Hernando De Soto, who slaughtered 3,000 Natives in what has been called one of the highest single-day body counts in all American history. Perhaps Dr. Seuss wasn't being entirely silly when he wrote about a line of cars called the Abrasion Contusion, all of them, it turned out, driven by specially trained drivers known as the Colliding Collusions. A 1965 Buick Skylark ad attempted to tantalize the would-be buyer by asking, "Ever prodded a throttle with 445 pound-feet of torque coiled tightly at the end of it? Do that with one of these and you can start billing yourself as the human cannonball." Forget the human cannonball; the human head, as Ralph Nader pointed out, would penetrate the windshield of the 1965 Buick Skylark at a speed as low as twelve miles per hour, a comment that prompted General Motors to hire a private detective in the hope of finding evidence to discredit him.

In the face of these suspicions, we are mown down like soldiers advancing into the wall of machine-gun fire, without protest, without demands that the war be brought to an end. We accept the slaughter. There are no pacifists in this war, no conscientious objectors, no talk of surrender. It is not clear who we would surrender *to*.

In recognition of this devastation, the United Nations and the World Health Organization in 2004 took the unprecedented step of declaring road death to be a "global crisis" and designated a day to address the problem. A road safety festival was held in Lebanon, a motorcycle helmet fashion show in Vietnam (not as frivolous as it might seem—in 2001, the number of motorcycles in Vietnam increased by nearly forty per cent, followed by a thirty-seven per cent increase in road deaths). Enormous amounts of data were generated to supplement the enormous amounts of data that had already been generated. Some of this information was summarized in a document called *World Report on Road Traffic Injury Prevention*, and it affirmed a great deal of what was already known and predicted.

Based on this and other research, it is now clear that seniors and children die disproportionately on the road. The elderly are twice as likely to be killed in a traffic accident as are the general public. Children from low-income families are five times more likely to be killed on the road than are children from high-income families. Ethnic minority children are at greater risk than others. Boys are twice as likely to be killed as girls; three-quarters of the people killed on the road worldwide are male. A child with a hearing difficulty is ten times more likely to be involved in a road accident than is a child whose hearing is not impaired. The casualty rate for children rises in the summer with the longer evenings. Twenty per cent of children killed on the road are killed while travelling to and from school. A child's greatest risk of a road accident occurs at the age of eleven or twelve. A girl of fifteen is three times more likely to be killed on the road than is a girl of thirteen. Twenty per cent of teenage boys killed on the road are killed while riding a bicycle.

This is the briefest sampling of the many ways that the consequences of road travel have been investigated. As a result of these investigations, there is no longer any doubt about how to significantly diminish road death: employ seat belts, airbags, rumble strips, traffic circles, speed bumps, divided highways, and photo radar; ban in-car telephone use; reduce the power output of motorcycle engines; increase the driving age from sixteen to eighteen; build segregated bicycle and pedestrian routes that connect to public transport; use flexible cable barriers as opposed to concrete ones; mandate daytime running lights for cars and motorcycles; install an alcohol ignition interlock system that detects alcohol on the breath of drivers. The list is long, comprehensive, and failproof. Implementing any item on it leads to quick and measurable results.

The modern road has been designed to facilitate speed, which has recently been identified as a leading factor in traffic injuries. Such injuries, it turns out, are proportional to the square of speed. Serious injury is proportional to the cube of speed. And fatal injury is proportional to the fourth power of speed. There are at least three "theoretical" approaches that link speed with "crash involvement," one of which is called the risk-homeostatis approach. In Saskatchewan, speed has been found to be a factor in 15.2 per cent of all casualty crashes. Limiting the speed of the vehicles that travel on the road is the oldest and most reliable method for reducing road carnage. When the city of Baden, Austria, instituted a thirty kilometres per hour or less speed limit on most of its roads in 1988, the number of road deaths dropped by sixty per cent.

There is no doubt that reduced speed on the road reduces the number of road deaths. The enforcement of those limits is costly, however, and it would seem that governments are not willing to bear the expense. At times, it appears the cost of improving road safety is considered frankly out of reach. In the end, it is easier and certainly cheaper to focus blame on the individual driver or pedestrian.

Despite the millions of people killed or wounded annually on U.S. roads, the automotive industry is notorious for prophesizing bankruptcy in the face of *any* safety innovation whatsoever. In the early years of the 20th century, General Motors was adamant that installing safety glass in their cars' windshields would cut unacceptably into profits. In the 1950s, the industry viewed mandatory seat belts with horror. Safety has "killed our business," Lee Iacocca once insisted. When the U.S. Congress considered implementing fuel efficiency standards, auto executives were quick to predict massive financial and unemployment problems. Now, with the U.S. government once again considering greater fuel efficiency in cars, auto executives are again opening briefcases containing documents that prove that more miles to the gallon will mean economic rigor mortis for the nation.

Despite the infinitely varied ways in which road safety can be approached, traffic safety experts agree, after half a century of intensive research, that along with reducing speed, the surest method of reducing vehicular death is to substantially cut down on the number of people who use cars and divert them to airplanes, trains, and buses instead. This is akin to suggesting that the number of drowning victims could be reduced by cutting down on the number of people who swim—perhaps by convincing them to play shuffleboard instead. It is hard to argue with. It is also directly opposed to an automotive industry determined to sell more cars than the year before.

Even more telling is that it ignores the deep personal tug of the road. No one has ever claimed to have discovered themselves, their country, or their destiny while being piloted through the stratosphere at 30,000 feet. This is not quality windshield time; it is hours and hours of shut windows and silly Hollywood movies. It is ultimately what Ruskin objected to about travelling by train, that it is not travelling at all; rather, it is "merely being *sent* . . . little different from being a parcel." This insistence on being a person and not a parcel is at the heart of the road's appeal, a stubborn insistence on a personal relationship to space and the landscape, and it is found almost exclusively, and most powerfully, on the road. The road is presumed to be dangerous. All voyages of discovery are dangerous, particularly ones of self-discovery.

=┤├=

Given all that is known about traffic accidents, experts predict that the situation is not about to improve. While reductions in road deaths are being achieved in high-income nations, poor and developing countries are suffering disproportionately. Rickshaws, mopeds, jitneys, motorcycles, and bicycles are appearing on the roads of developing nations in record numbers. In high-income Western nations, the electric or hybrid car signals the appearance of a new, friendlier, soundless automobile that comes up behind without warning and will take its toll particularly on the elderly or others whose hearing is no longer acute. It won't help that the driver will be talking on a cellphone and the children watching a television mounted above the back seat. By 2020, according to WHO, road injuries will move from ninth to third place in the ranking of world diseases.

As a mass slaughter, highway fatalities have escaped serious scrutiny by the media, making road deaths, in the opinion of British epidemiologist Ian Roberts, "the propaganda coup of the new millennium."

Each year, over 1.2 million dead, 50 million wounded.

The numbers are expected to increase by sixty-five per cent over the next twenty years.

ROADKILL

Until recently, the Kawartha Turtle Trauma Centre was located on Water Street in downtown Peterborough, Ontario—a name the street shares with the Water Street of St. John's, Newfoundland, thought to be the oldest street in North America. Before World War I, the merchants of Water Street, Newfoundland, employed twenty per cent of that province's workforce. The same cannot be said of Water Street in Peterborough, which today houses the Peterborough police department, the Peterborough legal centre, and, until recently, a number of evicted squatters who ended up camping on the front lawn of the Peterborough city hall until

the makeshift cabin they were sleeping in was mysteriously stolen.

Lately, the turtle rescue centre has left its Water Street home and moved several miles away to Lakeview, Susanna Moodie's old stomping ground, a pleasant and picturesque village perhaps more appropriate to the nursing of injured amphibians. There, with the help of two-ton epoxy, orthopedic screws, and dental braces, staff members attempt to heal the wounds and repair the fractures of a wide range of North American turtles.

Even though it is among the slowest creatures on the road, the turtle has done little to earn our displeasure. In Native mythology, the turtle is often a stand-in for the world itself, with the human race living on its back. The presence of a turtle in a local stream or river is typically seen as a testament to the health of that water. To discover a turtle-based act of outright aggression against man, we have to go back two and a half millennia, to the day an eagle mistook Aeschylus's bald head for a rock and, from a great height, released a turtle from its talons in an attempt to shatter its shell. The act is said to have resulted in the tragedian's death, making it the world's first recorded fatality involving a collision between a man and a turtle.

It would remain so until modern times.

What the Kawartha Turtle Trauma Centre reminds us is that, on the modern road, the turtle does not stand a chance. The female, attracted to the sandy shoulder of the highway as a prime spot to lay her eggs, is in danger both coming and going. Her babies are in danger from the moment they're born. And of course turtles of either sex are vulnerable due to the excruciating amount of time it takes for them to cross the road. It is perhaps this very slowness that tugs at our heart—the manifest unfairness of natural slowness pitted so brutally against the unnatural speed of the automobile. A study conducted on U.S. Interstate 27 quantifies the appallingly long odds facing any turtle foolish enough to cross a road, or at least *that* road: out of every hundred turtles that gives it a try, only two make it to the other side alive. Such numbers give force to University of Guelph biology professor Ronald Brooks's stated belief that unless something is done about the roadkill problem, the turtle as a species is not going to survive.

In the summer of 2004, in Indian River County, Florida, a foot-long Florida red-belly turtle attempted to cross Interstate 95. As it made its way onto the paved highway, it was hit by a truck and shot through the windshield of a van driven by a forty-five-year-old man on his way to visit his girlfriend. "When I looked up there was glass all over me and a turtle sitting beside me in my van," the driver said. The local paper made sure to describe the van driver as "shell shocked" but otherwise unharmed. Remarkably, the turtle was also uninjured and later released.

Such happy outcomes are rare.

As if things weren't bad enough for the road-going turtle, a study conducted in the Long Point region of Southern Ontario reveals that almost three per cent of drivers (men, mostly, but not always) deliberately go out of their way to target turtles and snakes on the road in an effort to kill them. Researchers placed fake decoys between the dashed lines down the centre of the road and recorded the number of vehicles that swerved out of their way to run them over. There's something kind of spooky about all this, not only the creepy three per cent with their fondness for indiscriminate slaughter, but to know that on any given road sociologists might be hidden in the bushes with their notebooks, watching us while we pilot our vehicles across the country. Such a scenario reverses the usual perceptual arrangements of the road as a place of privilege, a platform from which we observe the land while protected by the anonymity of tinted windows and motion. Instead, the road now threatens to become an investigative space on which we ourselves are studied, like lab rats deliberately placed in a maze.

To this point, the findings don't look too impressive. Of the 10,000 reptiles and amphibians killed every year on the Long Point Causeway, 300 of them are deliberately run down for the sheer fun of it. This is perhaps not so much road rage as road psychosis, where only in causing death does the driver feel truly alive, if only for a moment. One of the great and unforeseen tragedies of the road is the amount of physical power it gives the emotionally damaged, the psychologically impaired, and the run-of-the-mill screwups who have managed to pass a driving test. Whether we like it or not, the road is a democratic space, and along with our hopes and ambitions, it also facilitates the movement of extreme dysfunction.

Even without the murderous three per cent, the highway, as far as the wildlife goes, has proved to be as deadly as the Hudson's Bay Company ever was before it. Prior to the appearance of a nation-wide road network, a trek across Canada was often little more than an excuse to kill as many animals as possible. The poetical Henry Kelsey and his younger Native companion managed, in a six-day period during the summer of 1689, to shoot nine deer and a muskox, an animal no white person had ever seen before. But Kelsey was a virtual conservationist compared to the travellers who came later. When celebrated Canadian painter Paul Kane crossed Canada in 1846, he and his party shot everything in sight, including a massive wolf cut down for the simple reason that it was the largest wolf anyone had ever seen. They shot wolverines and eagles just to see what they tasted like. With the road in place, this type of killing moved away from the traveller and on to the vehicles in which they travel. From the animals' point of view, the difference hardly matters; for them, the massive network of roads *is* the second coming of the Hudson's Bay Company.

In 1970, when the last link of the Trans-Canada Highway was finally put in place, it meant that the animal kingdom faced a new and terrifying reality. The entire continent, from the Atlantic Ocean to the Pacific, was now completely and effectively divided in two by at least two lanes of traffic and in some cases sixteen. Often, these lanes themselves would be further fortified by impassable concrete barriers. The earth was split into two compartments that had no connection whatsoever with animal habitat or migratory patterns. A new, thoughtless, and impassable river had appeared on the earth—a form of physical schizophrenia in which the left is divided from the right, the north from the south, and the east from the west. Sometimes these chasms prove insurmountable, restricting the movement of animal populations, limiting the gene pool, and resulting in their isolation and even extinction.

The numbers are fragmentary, and often based on the assumption that for every animal verifiably killed on the road, three more manage to drag themselves off the highway to die in the bush. In the United States, researchers estimate that approximately one million animals are killed on the road—*each day*. This figure does not include animals killed by snowmobiles, all-terrain vehicles, or other off-road modes of transportation. On a relatively short section of highway in northern B.C., 4,000 animals are killed each year. To keep track of these casualties would require a staggeringly complex bureaucracy equal to and even exceeding the one in place to collate the human casualties.

The University of New Brunswick has conducted extensive studies on moose and deer–vehicle collisions in particular. The results, in their own words, are "sobering." The deer and moose–vehicle collision problem is sometimes referred to collectively as ungulate–vehicle collisions. It is known, for example, that one in every 796 New Brunswick drivers will strike a moose. From figures generated by the Michigan technology transfer centre, the University of New Brunswick has determined that a single deer killed on a New Brunswick road costs the economy $1,050. The same researchers concluded that the total number of ungulate–vehicle collisions in New Brunswick cost that province $14 million a year. This, like the study says, is a rather sobering figure coming out of a province that in the year 2000 had only slightly more than a half-million registered vehicles on the road and whose portion of the Trans-Canada, known as the Freedom Highway, is unpaved.

Freedom Highway or not, car rental agencies refuse to allow their cars to be driven on this road. Drivers who take it are advised to pack a satellite phone and will experience the creepy and undermining sensation of drifting from one side to the other as the round stones beneath the wheels shift the car left and right. Provincial signs warn you not to gut caribou by the side of the road. As a local woman explained to me, "People was just flinging the carcasses up into the trees, and it was stinking something awful. It was no good." To protect squeamish tourists, the signs now request that you gut the caribou fifty metres into the bush.

The moose is not any sort of an animal to encounter head on while driving a car. Weighing half a ton (1,000 pounds) and standing more than two metres (six feet) high, it is attracted to the highway by the road salt that it finds in abundance on the sides of the roads in spring. It can be found simply standing there with its head pointed upward, a massive rack of antlers branching into the sky. It is basking in the merciful openness of the Trans-Canada Highway, which cuts a swathe through the forest and allows a wind or breeze to sweep down and blow away the thick mantle of mosquitoes or black flies that cling to its back. This blanket of mosquitos can get so thick that it rises up and falls down again with each step the animal takes. Mosquito relief, and the abundance of road salt, make the road itself an attractive environment for a large number of animals. Since the moose stands considerably taller than the hoods of cars, during a collision its legs are knocked out from under it, rolling its body directly into the windshield or even the roof. It is not unheard of for the entire roof of a car to be stripped away by the force of such an impact. And because it stands at such a height, the headlights of oncoming cars pass beneath a moose's eyes. There is no sudden penetrating reflection, that eerie luminescent green glow that indicates there is something alive out there. There is nothing to be seen.

In New Brunswick, 250 vehicle–moose crashes a year are reported. Up to thirty per cent of moose "strikes" cause serious injury to the driver, with the most common injury sites being the head, face, and neck. In Quebec, 7,000 motorists a year make contact with, in descending order of frequency, a deer, a moose, a caribou, or a black bear. Some 1,500 of those crashes involve a moose.

The cost of vehicle–animal collisions is estimated in the United States to be $2,000 for every vehicle that is on the road. It seems that no end of actuarial-type calculations have gone into no end of intricately complex studies to prove just how impossibly large are the sums of money that animals are costing us. In Maine, New Brunswick's closest U.S. neighbour, the state suffers an economic loss of $32 million each year from more than 2,000 moose strikes and 12,000 deer strikes each year. In 2003, Manitoba Public Insurance paid out a record $20.6 million in vehicle collisions involving animals. In that year, some 300 Manitobans and more than 10,000 animals were injured in those accidents. In Ontario, one in every eighteen vehicle crashes are collisions involving a vehicle and an animal; every thirty-eight seconds, an animal and a vehicle collide.

Not surprisingly, appalling stories of animal–vehicle "crashes" abound. Years ago, I met a truck driver who simply refused to drive Northern Ontario at night. A Saskatchewan trucker described to me a harrowing scene in which he managed to stop his rig in front of a large moose positioned in the middle of the road. It was rutting season, and the animal charged. The driver sounded his horn but to no effect. The force of the impact hurled the animal up into the windshield, which somehow held, and the moose collapsed dead on the road.

The physics involved in animal–vehicle crashes are often bewildering. There are even formulas to account for those physics. They involve the speed in miles per second at which the animal enters the surface of the road, multiplied by the time in seconds between the vehicles crossing a common point on the road (vehicle separation), multiplied by the width or "impact zone" of the vehicle. For a turtle, the impact zone is equal to two tire widths. For a large animal such as a moose or coyote, the impact zone is equal to the full width of the vehicle.

While such equations may prove useful to researchers at the

research and development branch of the ministry of transportation, they are of little use to the pileated woodpecker, the winter wren, or the red-breasted nuthatch, which, after the construction of certain sections of Highway 401, encountered a serious loss of habitat. Wolf populations are particularly sensitive to new roads, sometimes vanishing entirely once a new road is built.

The fragmentation of the forest results in population declines among forest songbirds, many varieties of which require large, even immense forest interiors in order to breed. Roads force ground-based wildlife to attempt dangerous road crossings to forage and feed. It would seem there is no species at all that is immune to the impact of the road, and in ways that are often surprising. The sound of passing motorcycles can cause the premature emergence of the spade-footed toad. That familiar whooshing, almost tidal sound of passing traffic causes hearing losses in the sand lizard, which in turn decreases its ability to respond to predators. Reptiles and amphibians use the hard surface of the road to regulate their body temperatures. The road surface provides a welcome and inviting microclimate on which a vast range of creatures can raise their body temperatures once they have emerged from hibernation.

The road also has an enormous impact on fish populations and will continue to do so for some time yet. The fish is crucial to Canadian history, and fishing has become a national roadside industry, from the Bite Me Bait shop to the bait and tackle joints that provide "24-hour emergency service." "Most of my life I fished," says the sign mounted in a strip mall. "The rest of it I wasted."

While any new northern road opens up access to lakes previously reserved for the fly-in crowd, it's not necessarily the new road that poses the problem. The fisherman is an enterprising type, capable of flying in, walking in, or, if necessary, parachuting in to any remote spot where the big one might lurk. The problem often lies in roads that already exist—particularly in repairing the bridges. The sturgeon, for example, is the longest-living and largest freshwater fish in the world, and was once routinely found throughout Canada. It is central to the mythology of the Ojibwa, similar to the place of the buffalo among the Plains Indians, earning the name *Mishe-Nah'ma*, King of the Fishes. Sediment, dumped into riverbeds by bridge repairs, seriously impedes sturgeon spawning. Larval sturgeon drift downriver; that is how they enter the big lakes. Ideally, the modern, ethical, and environmentally responsible road crew would know exactly when, for each given river, stream or creek—1,525 tributaries drain into Lake Superior alone— such a larval drift takes place and would time its repairs to take place after the migration had finished. Or perhaps not. Perhaps they would attempt to get the job done at the lowest cost possible at a time that suited their schedule.

=⊣⊢=

In ways that eerily resemble the carnage inflicted on the human population, roadkill, in all its manifestations, generates little concern from lobby groups or the media and, strangely, is ignored by animal rights enthusiasts. A few years ago, a director of the Toronto-based lobby organization Animal Alliance of Canada admitted that the organization had no active campaign to address what is the leading cause of death among wildlife. Nor, to his knowledge, was there a single animal rights group in North America that did.

It is a strange oversight, as if the road is now perceived as an offshoot of nature itself, beyond our moral authority to fix, and certainly beyond the sphere of our blame. Animal rights groups are, in fact, conspicuous by their refusal to target the road as a primary or even tertiary threat to wildlife. More than a million animals a day are wiped out on the roads of North America, and not a word spoken, not a program in place. The road gets off without even a slap on the wrist. Getting it in the neck are KFC, McDonald's, multinationals, the furriers, and any Hollywood star thoughtless enough to be photographed in public wearing fur. It is an odd paradox, and it speaks to the ubiquity of the road, and the fact that even the most fervent of animal activists must surely put in countless miles on many a road.

The road, it seems, is morally a blank space, and whatever happens on it merely happens. We publish books titled *The Original Roadkill Cookbook*, which includes what the authors believe to be witty chapters on "pavement possum" or "hushed puppies." It has been said that the only highway on which animals are not killed is the information superhighway, but these books give the lie to that. There are artists who photograph roadkill, who make sculptures of it, who get out of their cars and paint fingernail polish onto the claws of dead animals. Roadkill artists, and comic book artists who specialize in roadkill, have created an industry.

If you want, you can get on the information highway and listen to them express their sensitive selves in a podcast or blog. "I believe that somewhere my human selves were guardians of human nature and the circle of life, because it is the strongest human drive that I have. It is synchronistic and symbiotic with

my maternal instincts and with self-sustaining logic." In other words, I am a woman who takes pictures of dead animals in the hope of selling them for lots of money.

We forgive this blather. We forgive the people who write it. We forgive the road, because apparently there is no other option. There is no *carkill*; it would hit too close to home. *Roadkill* is safer, as though the road itself destroyed these animals, not the cars, not the trucks driven by increasingly desperate drivers fuelled by wake-up pills and hurried on by anxieties about their jobs. This weird silence, almost paralysis, reminds us that the road is a complex place, and one that unpeels into finer and finer layers of meaning. Understanding any one of these meanings takes time, commitment, and financial resources that are probably not forthcoming. Realistically, how much money can we expect the district of Rainy River to spend investigating the premature emergence of the spade-footed toad when the district itself has serious difficulty financing the operation of a single ambulance? Currently we know more about the surface of the moon than we do about the effects of the road on the injury patterns of foxes, turtles, badgers, and porcupines. What little epidemiological evidence we do possess comes from police reports and the medical records of people who are killed or injured in animal–vehicle strikes.

In 2003, the Dene First Nation near Yellowknife brought some of these complexities to bear on the Bathurst Inlet Port and Road Project, a proposed 215-kilometre all-weather road through the caribou calving regions of Bathurst Inlet. A project description written by the road's promoters made the astounding claim that there would be "no interaction between road traffic and the elements of the terrestrial environment." It is mind-numbing that anyone could utter such nonsense, and, to their credit, the Dene Nation response managed to achieve a restrained level of disbelieving politeness when they asked, "Does the proponent expect there to be no animals road-killed for the life of the road?" Their questions highlight the many ways a road will intersect with what the promoters weirdly call the "terrestrial environment."

In expressing their concern about the impact of this road on the caribou herd, the Dene started at a point that not many people would have cause to think about. Before addressing the road itself, they wanted to know what amount of damage would be inflicted on the herd by the road construction crews, who would invariably unpack hunting rifles from their kits and start banging away at the caribou. It is against Canadian law to stand on a road and shoot an animal with a rifle, a bow, or a crossbow or to shoot across a road itself, but if the road is in the process of being built, presumably these restrictions are out the window. Of course, once the road is finished, a vast area will be opened up to the sports hunter and others, who would then have access to terrain traditionally denied to them. What effect, the Dene ask, will this have on the herd?

Then there is the matter of the dust—not only the dust thrown up by passing trucks, but the dust dispersed at the crushing sites required to build the road. Dust is an unavoidable consequence of roads, particularly remote and unpaved northern roads. This dust settles on neighbouring foliage. This dust-covered foliage is in turn eaten by the caribou, which, as the Dene Nation representatives point out, they have "relied on for countless generations to feed and clothe us." What is the effect of crushed stone dust on the digestive system of caribou? This is something that builders of roads should know. In fact, they need to be experts at it. In their public representations, Nuna Logistics and Kitikmeot Corporation, the companies behind the project, express nothing about the environment. Instead they rechristen the land in weird techno-speak, calling it SGP, or Slave Geological Province, make plenty of mention of diamonds and gold, and close with the not altogether reassuring motto, "If you build it they will come."

By contrast, the Dene First Nation has been forced to accept that the road has become a very complex space. It is forcibly bringing resource capitalism up against a culture that is still vested in the migration of wild animals and is interacting physically with traditional Aboriginal hunting culture, not only on the animals that will be hunted but on the very vegetation that those animals eat. The resolutions of these problems could conceivably require a team, or teams, of researchers armed with sophisticated equipment, heading off in all directions from a prototype crushing mill to determine the rates of dust dispersal across a boreal landscape when the winds are blowing at ten kilometres an hour. And what about when it blows at fifteen kilometres an hour, or sixteen, or thirty-five? These are complex and laborious calculations, and they can only get more so once the trucks themselves actually start rolling down the highway.

Caribou also migrate. In fact, they migrate with great determination. With the building of this road, the herd for the first time will join the wildlife of southern Canada, and most of the rest of the world, in that they too will be faced with a long and winding chasm that separates one side from the other. That chasm will be packed with massive, swift-moving transports driven by men facing stiff pressure to get to their destination as fast as possible. The

Dene First Nation would seem justified in asking that the road proponent "show the locations of all traditional caribou trails that the
proposed road will bisect."

There are many sides to every road, and while a new road would
presumably bring employment and great wealth to De Beers (and
its shareholders) and other resource companies, it could very well
impoverish the people who live in the land that surrounds it.
What, the Dene ask, would be the consequences of the caribou migration being deflected in ways that can't be predicted, forcing the
herd further away from traditional hunting areas? These are tough
questions, and they stand in stark contrast to Thomas Wilby's glorious and uncomplicated confidence that a new road will "reform
the man, reform the housewife, transform the children."

=||=

No doubt the reformed man, woman, and child would want to
help minimize the effects of the roads they travel on, and would
gladly do what they could to reduce the destruction of the natural environment and the suffering of animals. It is perhaps unrea-
sonable, however, to expect us to do as much as the Tweed Valley
Wildlife Carers would have us do when it comes to protecting the
ringtail and the brushtail possum. While many possums are killed
on our roads each night, it is their joeys that go unnoticed. A baby
possum can live in its dead mother's pouch for several days. The
advice of the Tweed Valley Life Carers is that we stop the car, move
the carcass well back from the road, then check the pouches of
any dead marsupial that we have run down. Should we find a joey
in the pouch of a dead possum, we are to "wrap it in a beanie,

cloth bag, sock or towel," put it next to our skin to keep it warm, and contact our local animal rescue society. With nearly three per cent of the population deliberately veering out of their way to kill animals on the road, it is heartening and even reasonable to think that an equivalent three per cent, after moving an animal carcass back from the road, will then put their fingers into the pouch of a dead possum to check for a living joey.

Failing that, there are other options for reducing the road's impact on wildlife. In Europe, there are times when a road is closed to traffic to permit unusually active wildlife migrations. There are times in Canada when a driver might wish for such a strategy, particularly, for example, during a massive frog migration.

These migrations tend to occur at night, almost always after a rainfall. The phenomenon, at first and even second glance, appears as a visual anomaly, a weird, brief shimmer on the road surface, a glint of something small in the headlights. After a few moments, you become aware that the entire road, from shoulder to shoulder, is writhing. The sensation is nightmarish, and becomes more so when you realize that the road is entirely slick with toads and frogs of all varieties. An apocalyptic vision from the Old Testament is appearing in front of your vehicle. The road is wet, and the headlights of the car behind you glare in the rearview mirror, urging you to go faster. Against your own better judgment, you calculate the sheer numbers of frogs that you're slaughtering. It seems impossible that there are this many frogs on the entire planet. You watch, completely helpless, as they expire beneath your wheels, popping, exploding by the dozens, by the hundreds, the thousands. Before this traumatizing ride is over, the frog will be extinct—you just know it. And it will be all your fault. It's an experience that many Canadian drivers have had. It is not one that anyone quickly forgets.

From frogs to possums to deer by the thousands, to moose, raccoons, porcupines, and bears, from sand lizards to foxes and every other living creature that moves or flies across the earth, the road, at every moment, entwines them in the possibility of catastrophic and sudden death. There are times when this death is almost obscenely balletic, a gruesome dance in which turtles are hurled like bullets through the windshields of moving cars and massive ungulates stand motionless, sadly watching the vehicle that will take their life away. According to Transport Canada, ten per cent of animals struck on the road are struck with such force that they become airborne and are sent hurtling through the windshield of an oncoming vehicle, often killing its driver or passenger or both. This is a common road experience: that loud thump made by contact with a deer you never saw, for the simple reason that the deer was in another lane and another vehicle smacked it across four lanes of highway into the passenger side of your car.

The deer is at the heart of the North American roadkill problem, so much so that the state of Michigan, for example, uses roadkill statistics to determine its state-wide deer population. There are somewhat less than half a million deer killed each year on the roads of the United States. For an animal that is so fleet on the land, so utterly elegant in the way it turns its long, shining neck with the shoulders, torso, and rest of the body following, the deer is nothing short of goofy on the road. On the hard surface, it stands as inelegant and hobbled as a two-year-old girl who has managed to put on her mother's high heels. It even looks like that, the feet turned inward, the perplexed appearance on the face, as if asking, "What is this thing"? One can only wonder what it feels like underfoot, this hard surface that is without give, on which the soft cloven hoof burns in the summer heat. The flight response of the deer is all wrong for the road. Weirdly, a deer will try to out-run your car, and there is no shortage of road travellers who have had the sensation of looking out either the passenger's or driver's window to see a deer in full desperate gallop, both driver and deer trying to pull ahead of each other, the deer, in that panicked mo-ment, turning its head to make eye contact with you.

Other times, the deer are so numerous they don't even bother to run. At night, driving the Sibley Peninsula beneath a sickle moon, I watched the deer pulse through the forest onto the road, revealing the imperial, disdainful motion of the bucks, unwilling to hurry out of the way, the does nimbly picking their routes. To the left, the right, the middle, a dozen of them, two dozen. The tight forest of the peninsula burst with deer, parting the under-brush, crowding the road, until the deer seemed to outnumber the neighbouring 1,300 campers nestled into Sleeping Giant Provin-cial Park. The deer streamed through the twilight that in early July feels as if it extends until midnight. This is what the road can give access to, a dangerous and stunning animal otherness. At twenty-five kilometres an hour, with the headlights on, the deer seem to be passing through here like a caribou herd. The car is almost nudging them with its fenders, parting a way through their mass.

While animal rights groups might be free to ignore the daily slaughter of wildlife on the roads of North America, other seg-ments of society are not. Insurance companies, road builders, and even automobile manufacturers are heavily invested in providing some sort of solution to the million-plus animals killed on the roads of the continent each day. Various solutions have been recommended and some of them implemented. One of the first that gets bandied about is an increase in the annual cull numbers. This would allow hunters to kill more animals, reducing the numbers and consequently reducing the number of animals available to wander out on the road and do damage to a moving vehicle. This rings of the old Vietnam pacification strategy: to save the animals, it is first necessary to kill the animals.

According to experts, deer and moose herds are in a period of revitalization, their numbers increasing at the same time that their habitat is disappearing due to, among other things, road expansion. The number of cars, trucks, and motorcycles on those roads is also increasing. None of this is good news for either animal or driver. Suggesting that we kill more animals to reduce the number of animal–vehicle strikes is no more unlikely than suggesting that we reduce car accidents by reducing the number of people in cars. It will work, but the increased culling of animals does involve sending more people out into the bush with high-powered rifles.

The first and perhaps most radical solution is to slow down. To slow down is to fly in the face of everything the road stands for and may in fact be culturally impossible. Slow is bad. Slow is the past—not the romantic past of "home-cooked meals" but of Internet connections that make you wait forever and gratifications that for some reason are hardly ever immediate. To encourage this slowing down on the part of the driver is a series of black-on-yellow signs that symbolically explain that you are entering a high-risk animal collision area. Signs are known as passive

196 / PETER UNWIN

warnings—and are notably unsuccessful. It is estimated that sixty per cent of drivers actually don't see them. Other low-tech solutions include "vegetative palatability" strategies, seeding roadsides with plants that moose and deer do not eat. Fencing is another relatively low-tech solution that is entirely effective and would reduce animal collisions by ninety-seven to ninety-nine per cent. It would also disastrously fragment habitats, split herds, obliterate migratory patterns, and prevent animals from escaping from hunter animals, which, it now seems, are fully capable of using fences to corner and trap their prey. To fence both sides of the highway costs between $40,000 and $80,000 per kilometre, and that figure does not includes maintenance costs, which are high, and endless.

Overpasses and underpasses have long been used as a solution in national parks such as Banff, which has more than twenty of them in place. They cost a fortune, require detailed engineering, and sometimes provide a one-stop snacking location for hungry predators. They also seem to work, and to work very well. Another solution is the deer whistle. There is no formal evidence to suggest that these whistles, which are mounted on the front of vehicles and emit a high-pitched sound inaudible to humans, actually work, although many drivers swear by them.

A Canadian company, International Road Dynamics, has developed a sensor system to be placed at known roadside trouble spots. These sensors alert deer to approaching traffic with a series of flashing lights and high-frequency sounds. They are, in effect, traffic signals for animals and aim to divert the animal from the road before the oncoming vehicle actually arrives. In the absence of traffic, the signals are inactive and the animal is not discouraged from crossing the road.

The Cadillac DeVille, built by General Motors, used infrared night vision technology developed by the U.S. army to spot tanks in Iraq. This piece of technology came as a stand-alone option and was said to enable a driver to react more quickly in the presence of an animal. We have now reached the point of using NASA-developed technology in an attempt to stem the destructive interaction between vehicle and animal.

Until the ideal high- or low-tech solution has been engineered, the animals who find themselves on the road will have to continue to rely on blind luck. In the late spring of 2000, driving southbound on the 400 below Algonquin Park, I was swept forward in the mad, overamped traffic of that particular stretch of road. The rain was intense, the fog deep and blinding. All at once, something appeared out of it, a huge grey presence floating forward, appearing in front me the way a freighter emerges from the fog. A fully antlered moose towered above the vehicles, nudging across eight intense and teeming lanes of red-tail-light traffic. Breasting one lane after another, it slowly, wearily, as if parting the vehicles before it, picked its body over a concrete barrier separating the northbound from the southbound lanes. Then, like a dream, the animal dissolved in the rain and fog and was gone, moving stately, unhurried, across the final four lanes, down the slope, and into the woods—alive.

READING THE ROAD

From the Trans-Canada Highway, Garden River, Ontario, is a small, pleasant settlement that appears slightly sunken, as though the village has given way to the weight and density of the swampy foliage, the rock, and the trees. The erratic scatter of the buildings tells you that you've entered a First Nations reserve, as do the signs: Ojibway Tent and Trailer Park; Wigwaus Street; Oji-Cree Meats. In case there is any doubt, two gigantic sculpted arrows, sticking from the earth and extending three stories into the air, seal the deal.

The fishing is good here in Garden River. So is the gardening, and so, it seems, is the baseball. In 1972, the first All-Ontario Aboriginal Fastball Championship was held in Garden River, with the

Moravian of the Thames team going home with the trophy. A roughshod baseball diamond is visible from the highway, and like many of the baseball pitches of deep Canada, it is crisscrossed with wire fencing and history. At times, the bags and ball are left on the diamond for the next players. Sometimes discarded church pews stand in for benches.

Something else is visible from the highway as well—readily visible: four words hand-painted in tall, skinny white letters on the side of the train trestle. The words have been there for many years, and they state, without equivocation, THIS IS INDIAN LAND. For a long time the *is* was smudged, having been replaced with the word *was*, still faintly visible beneath another layer of paint: "This *was* Indian land." Further smudging is evident to the right of the word *land*, further edits and further erasures. To the original graffiti, "This is Indian land," someone had predictably added "and smells like it too." More than one layer of smudging and defacement is visible, and it is clear that the battle between *was* and *is* has been going on for some time here.

Today, the sign is clear and defiant. This *is* Indian land. The letters stand ten feet tall and freshly painted, as if a new Native confidence has swept the Earth, or at least the village of Garden River. There is no more "was" on display here, only the "is," the here and now. A Canadian flag has been painted at one end, indicating that to be Native and to be Canadian are often the same thing. The fact that the red maple leaf in the middle of the flag is painted with a Native male face at its centre feels almost ominously defiant, but against whom this defiance is directed is not clear.

It is hard to imagine another location in the country where a driver can pass a piece of graffiti that so entirely encapsulates and

grapples with a nation's history. In
this case, it's a conflict fought on
the roadside, on the ground, not in
lecture halls or professorial offices
but most likely by teenagers on bicycles, local kids with resentments,

fired up equally by the desire to dangle from a train bridge, to
demonstrate their bravery, and to engage in political action. To
stop your car here, to get out and stand on the middle of this
bridge, is to stand in the exact centre of two solitudes: not Hugh
MacLennan's *Two Solitudes*, which takes it for granted that the
Canadian divide is between two European cultures, but the two
actual solitudes of Canada: the non-Native and Native, the *us* and
them, the *is* and the *was*.

This great conflict is the touchstone of Canada and goes back
ten centuries to the days when the Mi'kmaq of the Miramichi were
convincing Leif and Thorvald Erickson that it might be good idea
to get in their ships and go back home. From Miramichi to Ipper-
wash to Caledonia, this conflict shows every sign of going on for
a long time yet.

This is Indian land. The power of these four words lies in their
disarming frankness and their undeniablity. Garden River has been
a reserve since 1850, when this entire area was under the leadership of Chief Shingwauk, the man reputed to have shot dead the
American soldier who killed General Brock at the Battle of Queenston Heights. The graffiti is magnified by the sheer visibility of the
statement: it is almost impossible to cross Canada by road without
reading it, making it perhaps *the* most well-known piece of graffiti
in the country. When I show this slide in lectures and readings, it

is met, without exception, by a gasp from at least someone in the audience. "I've seen that," a voice pipes up, with emotion. One man, a travelling salesman, was particularly moved. "My God," he said, "I've been driving past that for years."

The emotion expressed is a result of finding out that history is there in the same room with you, and very much alive. The road facilitates this closeness, insisting that history is not only something we read but something physical. It works its way through the windshield and into the car. It is there on a train bridge at Garden River. We can't escape the impact, the sudden realization that a piece of defaced graffiti alternating between *this is* and *this was* is history itself, and not a minor subchapter but its most vital core. This is what is shocking: the profusion of history, so much of it that it crowds itself against the very road itself.

=|=

With the window open, the crackling of rubber on paved blacktop emanates from everywhere at once. Eventually the sound becomes deafening, the window is rolled up, and the enveloping white static of the highway is entirely gone, as if sealed away in a vacuum. There is no longer any sense of motion; only the signs whip by, and those poles, those wooden crosses that resemble so many crucifixes, joined by a sinew of cable, stretching on forever. Without them flashing by, there would be no indication that anything is moving at all. Up closer are the signs:

Wasaga Beach
Nottawasaga

Wahta Mohawk Territory
Iroquois Cranberry Growers Pow Wow
Shawanaga First Nation
Magnetawan First Nation

Occasionally the signs are interspersed with others in a different language, English or French, mostly English, which seems
strangely out of place and unconvincing, as if the language itself
lacks the subtlety to help us deal with this land. For the most part,
the book of the Canadian road is written in the Native languages.
As the traveller heads west, out across the Prairies and into the
mountains, the signs change. The vast Ojibwa empire is left behind, and with it the Algonquian-based language group. We reach
the land and the language of a different Native group, with that
language's X's and Q's and apostrophes.

As we ride the road, we read this book and learn from it. Any
car ride across central Canada is a daily lesson in the language of
the Ojibwa. We have long ago absorbed the meaning of *muskeg* and
deduce that *Muskoka* will perhaps reveal similar territory. Out of the
swamp (muskeg) rise the *mosquitoes*. In the reeds wait the massive
musky, or *muskellunge*, that fishermen from all over the world come
to hunt and, by law, release. The road advances us through this dictionary, from Mississauga to Mississippi, increasing our word hoard
with every mile. Unlike the United States, where so many Native
place names have been anglicized, in Canada we still largely drive
a country in its original tongue, riding its language through the
rock, the earth, and the muskeg. To change the name of these places
is to lose the origins and the continuity of who we are, and to
wound our identity. In the past two decades, Canada has under-

gone a widespread campaign to return place names to their original language, a type of nationwide act of Peace and Reconciliation in which we attempt to heal ourselves from wanton acts of naming.

One way or another, the road demands that we read it. Like a book, the road takes us to another place, provides escape, entertainment, diversion, perhaps transformation and enlightenment. Like many books, it is often badly written, boring, and constructed for the sole and unlikely reason of making money for someone. To travel the road is to participate in reading: the linear motion of going down the page, going down the road, the eyes swivelling left and right across the windshield. In driving, as in reading, one can go numb, with only the odd phrase or image filtering through and entering the consciousness. The road, like the book, is someone else's attempt to fashion reality. Close it for a moment, and there is the wallpaper that you and your partner nearly came to blows over, the scattering of children's toys, and the unread sports section of the newspaper. The road brings its own sense of sameness, but it is one that can change very quickly with the sudden appearance of a stag with a fourteen-point rack, standing calmly in the middle of the road and looking at you with stunning indifference.

A moment later, we are returned to the unending, lonely skyline of serrated treetops. Beneath it, on the ground, the chief architectural achievements are the tin shed, the Frost fencing, abandoned trucks sticking out from the grass, and the rusted air compressors that litter the fields. These things form the unremarked landscape, the one that landscape painters never render, the one that resolutely never gets mentioned in tour books or printed on postcards or in coffee table books, always shunted to the side and replaced instead by the majestic peaks of the Rockies, the mighty rivers, etc. Yet these are the true icons of the Canadian road, ruled over by the also-never-depicted massive hydro pylons that march across the land: gigantic skeletal robots that carry down on their shoulders the power lines from the hydroelectric stations of the North, powering our TVs, our stoves, our Xboxes.

If we stop the car and get out, we are struck at once by the stunning silence of the highway, as if the road itself, like a fresh snowfall, has muffled all sound. The prevailing sense is one of loneliness: the extreme loneliness of wind and rock, the mobs of trees, all of them whispering in a language that is foreign to us, impenetrable, praying to God, as Grey Owl put it, to be saved from the timberman. Absent, at least for a moment, is what the poet Robert Lowell called "traffic with its unbroken snore." There's a white-throated sparrow whistling invisibly from the bush. Then comes the crescendo and decrescendo of a passing truck, sounding remarkably at first like a fighter plane, then like the wind in the tops of the trees. Eventually it is gone and silence returns. We expect this silence and sense in it a return to the past, when these nasty, dirty vehicles didn't exist and travel was a pastoral romance of horse and buggy, water and wood, and the road sounded very different: the plunk of paddles against water, the singing of French, English and Métis songs, the sound of a breaking twig, or the thump of the paddle steamer.

In such a moment, it is easy to forget that the road has been a dirty and noisy space for a long time. The legendary Red River cart, constructed entirely of wood and leather, made such an ear-splitting screech that it was audible miles away. In keeping with its close-to-earth construction, the axles of a Red River cart were often greased with frogs, worms, or whatever reptile happened to be available in the nearest pond. The Persian traveller Mizru Abu Taleb, on a whirlwind European tour, remarked, "From the day I arrived in Dublin, till I quitted Paris the sound of coach wheels were never out of my ear." He was travelling in the noise-polluted year of 1752. In ancient Rome, Caesar once instituted a ban on daytime chariot use, exempting only those vehicles transporting construction material to the temples of the gods. That old-time clatter is now replaced by a tidal sound, the hush-hushing of an oncoming car, like a wave breaking over us. The slish of car tires on wet pavement. Now there are countries in the world where it is barely possible to get out of auditory range of a passing car or truck. This is the new song of the open road. We do not sing it. It is sung to us.

Outside the car, once that deep silence has been accepted, there is nothing to do but examine the road and what surrounds it. The pebbled surface of the pavement gives way to gravel shoulders and the band of grass that separates the highway from the rest of the world. First seen is a speckling of devil's paintbrush, black-eyed Susans, the purple vetch, and the blueberries with their waxy leaves. On closer inspection, you see cigarette butts; in particular, cigarette *filters*, generations of them, extending back a half-century or longer, brands that no longer exist, the fiberglass filters that last a millennium. Here are the Sweet Caporals of our forefathers, the brutal Export A's that we remember seeing twisted arrogantly beneath the sleeve of a white-T-shirted young man with a hint of a James Dean haircut—a young man who died a martyr to the road. The smokes have been inserted in the sleeve because the blue jeans are too tight to accommodate them.

Smoking is allowed on the road, even encouraged, as indicated by the mantle of butts that lie over the ground. Further afield, blown there by the slipstream of each passing vehicle, are the empty cigarette packages. The colour has been bleached out of them long ago, and they look like large teeth knocked to the ground in the brutal fight against distance. As with the great trans-Canadian paddles of the voyageurs, the road can be measured in tobacco. Five smokes between Brandon and Winnipeg. Five pipes between the Soo and Grand Portage. Those nicotinic trances, vividly preserved in the paintings of Frances Anne Hopkins, are filled with a glamour that is denied the modern smoker in a car. But essentially they are the same, a brief moment of distraction to mark time and distance in the numbing passage of space.

The culmination of those passages is, if not a masterpiece, at least a great and shaggy story, the biggest and the most meaningful book we have managed to write. For all of its noise, for all of the massacres that continue to take place on it, the road is a mark of civilization: a long sinuous line unrolling from one end of the country to the other, and allowing us entry to the spaces in between. It is the truest measure of a country that we have, and the means by which we comprehend its size. The closest we will come to actually feeling it in our bones is to drive it, to feel the passage of miles vibrating at the base of our skull.

＝╪╞

There is grandeur to this road that no number of cheesy billboards can completely obliterate. Those billboards are themselves crucial chapters in the book of the road. Although they didn't begin to block out the landscape until the end of World War II, they now combine with the staggering amount of signage that bristles from the roadside to form a library of desperate messages urging us to buy something, to go somewhere, to believe something. Many of these billboards are mere skeletal wood frames, erected by companies named Ernie's or Arrow's, propped up against the rock like a cheap Hollywood set and rented by the month. We read them all, even the most obscure, sometimes not even knowing we're doing it. It's a way of marking time, a method of entertaining ourselves in the act of travelling.

These signs exist in competition with what is loosely called "nature" or "the landscape," distracting us from the Queen Anne's lace that bobs on the side of the road, cheeky as can-can dancers. Roadside signs have become so numerous that they're part of the landscape itself. In Canada, their mass appearance began in 1913, when the recently formed Ontario Motor League began a campaign of erecting signs to aid the motorist. Over the next twenty-five years, the league alone would put up more than 200,000 road signs, which in itself would seem like enough to satisfy the needs of any driver. In fact, it was just the beginning. Today, road signs are erected out of habit, some of them implausibly ridiculous signs, like novels that should never have been written: signs that say, "You are now entering the eastern Ontario tourist region." Strangely, there is no sign that reads, "You are now *leaving* the eastern Ontario tourist region." Once you enter a tourist region, there is no leaving it.

Tourists, it would seem, are gullible, childlike creatures who require no end of written roadside information, and a great deal of the book of the road is written for them. A sign at Bonnechere Provincial Park in Ontario indicates just how cautiously we need to proceed should one of them wander anywhere near the road.

It was understood early on that not all riders would know how to read, certainly not in English, so a system of symbols was employed, beginning with the traffic light, the first of which appeared in Detroit in 1910.

Now everyone is in on it. From three levels of government to graffiti artists, anti-abortionists, Christians, and novel writers, the road has become a literal information superhighway that integrates text and non-literary symbols into a mind-numbing display of information. If the Parry Sound hospital needs a new CT scanner, there will be signs on the Trans-Canada letting you know and urging you to dig deep. In Northern Ontario, a large number of signs urge you to consider the pain of sexually abused children: Save the Children. Stop Sexual Abuse. The words whip by, but it isn't clear to me, with my foot on the accelerator and my hands on the steering wheel, how exactly I am at this moment supposed to save the children or stop sexual abuse. Probably I'm supposed to give money to someone. Nearly every one of these countless written and painted signs come down to this: give us your money. "Pregnant? Need food for a healthy baby?" There's a number to call. "Know in your heart that Christ is Lord."

And all of these roads take us through God's Country—the signs tell us as much, or they speak of the difficulty involved in living the spiritual life of the road. One sign, planted on the lawn in front of a motel on Highway 62, said simply

Welcome to God's Country
No Vacancy

Often it isn't clear what the sign means or what it's doing there in the first place. Today, the roadsides of Canada are towered over by the ubiquitous inukshuk. This is a recent phenomenon: the virtual colonization of the road by these human-shaped stone monuments. They are found planted on the rock cuts of the Trans-Canada and on any road where rock is prevalent, and they constitute a Canadian equivalent to "Kilroy was here." These structures have become an industry, and we are cheerfully informed by the Oriana Communications website that these inukshuks "have captured the imagination of Canadians from coast to coast." There is no mention of cultural appropriation, even though the recent appearance of these symbols is the largest and most unremarked cultural appropriation the land has ever experienced. The inukshuk has been happily interpreted as "a symbol of friendship," although who gave it that interpretation, or where that connotation comes from, is never made clear. *Inukshuk* means, we are told "to act in the capacity of a human." Or perhaps it means "in the likeness of a human." Miniature inukshuks can be bought at every tourist trap the roadside has to offer, including the Busy Bee outside the town of Nairn Centre on Highway 17, where they are sold alongside the made-in-Canada "noiseless" hunting vest ($14.99). Even the *Canadian Encyclopedia* urges us to "make your own inukshuk in a flash!" One wireless company, named Inukshuk Wireless Inc., informs us that the inukshuk is also "a welcome guide to

travellers on the Internet." It is a symbol of "leadership . . . cooperation . . . the human spirit." It helps the hunter fell the caribou and the fisherman catch the fish. It prevents us from getting lost. It memorializes our deceased loved ones. It commemorates the importance of friendship and represents "safety and nourishment, trust and reassurance." Like the road itself, there is nothing that the inukshuk does not symbolize. Need a symbol for International Youth Day? Slap an inukshuk on it. Vancouver Olympics coming up? Quick, haul out the inukshuk. When Olympic officials did precisely that, First Nations groups considered walking out in protest. These structures, long ago, were thought to be instrumental in the crucial slaughter of the caribou. Now they have been entirely sanitized and turned into a cool universal marketing device, Happy Faces made of rock that mean whatever anyone wants them to mean, and as a consequence mean nothing at all.

The sudden appearance of these things on the roads of Canada has provided the traveller with an accessible and comforting sense of the exotic. They provide a continuous roadside attraction, hidden and even protected under the guise of First Nations culture, offering the authenticity that the road is expected to deliver but that we somehow can't deliver to ourselves. "I was here," or "Ted loves Veronica always," just don't cut it. Even on the road, we have come to accept that the authentic is something that exists outside of us. Despite being decidedly non-Inuit, the rarely seen drivers who stop their cars, scramble to the top of a rock cut, and quickly assembly their wobbly interpretation of an inukshuk are in that moment searching for a connection to the land that's denied them. It is their way of experiencing the Arctic without having to freeze to death or eat the raw flesh of a walrus.

Ministry of transport road crews seem to have granted these structures a sacred Aboriginal meaning; road crews, in fact, are under orders not to dismantle them, providing they don't show any imminent sign off falling off the top of a rock or rolling into a "live" lane. This attitude stands in stark contrast to that of Canadian park officials, who are also facing an invasion of inukshuks. Park workers on Highway 69 near the French River Visitor Centre report dismantling as many as thirty of them in a single day.

=⊣⊢

The core of Canadian road signage is traffic-based and concerns itself with regulations, warnings, temporary conditions, and directions. This vast, complex, symbolic, and colour-coded language is made up of images we assimilate over time, like a new language we absorb without thinking about. Through long exposure, we come to accept that the sign bearing a green circle means we must do the activity described in that ring, or at least consider doing it. That a red triangle with white in the middle means "yield" is something we no longer have to think about. Travelling at 110 kilometres an hour, we barely have *time* to think about it. We have learned it, and we yield or we don't. The signs are barely noticed. A rural American driver once insisted he didn't need signs to tell him how fast to go, or even, for that matter, a speedometer in his vehicle. At ten miles an hour, the fenders rattled; at twenty miles an hour, the transmission growled; and at thirty miles per hour, his false teeth fell out.

The modern road with its sleek blacktop surface has put an end to such folksy understanding, and as a consequence the road is now a cautionary place that requires no end of warnings. Like a nervous parent, it is forever warning us against just about everything. Typically, these warnings take the form of yellow triangles or diamonds that tell us, without words, that there is a bump ahead,

that the pavement is slippery when wet, that the paved surface is ending, that there is a sharp bend ahead, or that the bridge in front of us won't accommodate two vehicles side by side. There are countless signs indicating just what a treacherous and catastrophic place the road can be, with its soft shoulders, steep hills, and wet surfaces, with workmen ahead or with children at play. There is the Watch for Falling Rock sign, and on rarer occasions the Watch for Falling Ice sign. For whatever reason, there are no signs that explain what to do if we see any, giving rise to a favourite and much repeated complaint of my father's during the drives of my childhood: "They tell you to watch for falling rock," he grumbled, "but they never tell you what to do when you see any."

Behind us, other road signs have flashed so often that we have absorbed them into the vast clutter of memory. They seem to reach back into childhood and sometimes feature children predominantly displayed on them. Of course, it's impossible for these signs not to reflect the cultural ideals of the times: the gender assumptions, the role of boys, the role of girls. My favourite is the boy at play, for he is precisely and determinedly that: a boy running flat out, in mad, ecstatic pursuit of that ball, of his own ability to move swiftly over the land. Look at those feet: platforms that root the boy to the earth and to the road that will take him on so many adventures. Was childhood ever this free and glorious? Yes, in fact, for a brief moment it was, back when the road was merely a place we landed on, in those rare moments when we were not airborne.

When written in the book of the road, "children at play" invariably means "boys at play." Compare him to his rarely seen sister—there she is in the School Crossing sign, cautiously moving forward, no doubt looking right and left. She is nestled in the protective arm of her brother or father, who towers above her. Clearly, she is not to about to do anything impulsive, no chasing after silly balls for her. She is on her way forward, to her education, to responsibility. Soon it will be her job to look after us.

She seems to sense this, and perhaps that older, larger male figure is not so much protecting her as pushing her forward, making sure she doesn't give in to the urge to be airborne and to chase that ball along with that carefree boy with the handsome, strong legs. In fact, it isn't clear how this couple is moving forward at all, for in an astonishing and almost obscene oversight, they have no hands and, more pointedly, no feet!

What exactly is going on when a road sign depicts people as having no feet? Is the message really that the road has somehow detached us from the earth itself, taking away our ability to walk, to know the earth one step at a time? Leaving a Thunder Bay hotel one morning, I asked the desk clerk how long it would take me to walk to the bus terminal. She thought about it carefully and said, "Ten minutes." Twenty-five minutes later, I began to jog. At forty-five minutes, I arrived just in time to miss my bus. She knew her city inside out, but she had lost any sense of the pace of the

human step. Our contact with the earth is mediated by pavement or concrete sidewalks, divorced even further from us by the vehicles that hustle us about. To go anywhere, even to school, especially to school, we must huddle together, sisters pressed to the safety of their brothers' arms. Hand-less, footless, incapable of touching the face of the earth, our children drift forward waiting to be buffeted by the cars whose rubber feet very much touch the ground and whose gleaming hoods cut forcibly through the air.

When not warning us, it is often the function of road signs to give advice. On the hard surface travels the most mobile and the most captive of consumers, the tourist trapped in a car, and one of the first assumptions made about such folks is that they are in desperate need of advice. "When you are away from home," warns the Standard Oil Company, "you often want advice." They forget that in taking to the road, we are just as often trying to get as far away from advice as we can, especially from that crushing variety known as "well-intentioned." Standard Oil assumes that no self-respecting tourist would take to the road without a "Tourist Information Kit" containing plenty of "Standard Personalized Information," information obtained, not surprisingly, from Standard Oil.

The road, the signs tell us, is in desperate need of the tourist, just as a Canadian book—this book, for example—is in need of a reader. All those twelve-inch hot dogs, those Fries Ahead signs nailed to trees, those billboards that promote the joys of cosmetic surgery, and the blue metallic signs with raised letters that explain, for example, that the Great Dynamite Explosion of 1885 took place right here on Highway 28 just north of County Rd #4, killing Messers Morton and Simmons and their steed, leaving only "fragments of the men, horses and wagon." No one is in control of this great book. Anyone can add to it. And nearly everyone has.

=⊨=

To turn the road into one endless consumer space, it is necessary to give the money-laden tourist something to gape at. One of the first efforts to accomplish this took place on the Via Appia, considered in its time the longest road in the world. In 70 BC, along the side of the road, more than 6,000 followers of Spartacus were crucified and their bodies left to hang for decades, representing perhaps the first time in history that the road had been exploited as a premium advertising space.

Two thousand years later, we find ourselves witness to a different spectacle: the bizarre and delightful freak show known as the roadside attraction. Nearly 900 of these constructions demand our attention from one coast to another, with many more appearing each year. From the Drain Chicken of Tweed, Ontario, to the Giant Pinto Bean of Bow Island, Alberta, these typically cartoonish figures seemed to be aimed at children, and almost without exception signal that some restaurant or roadside eatery is close by. Fries can be had, and the ubiquitous and patriotic serving of coleslaw. Your children need to pee? Of course they do. Stop and take in the World's Largest Perogy in Glendon, Alberta, population 421 and still declining.

These schmaltzy folk constructions become a way of branding a town. Towns do it eagerly, desperately, as a way of putting themselves on the roadmap. Although Glendon, Alberta, doesn't merit a mention in the *Canadian Encyclopedia*, Wikipedia is glad to include it, spending most of its brief reference on, of course, the world's largest perogy.

Food is a staple of the roadside attraction. If you're driving through Mundare, Alberta, you could, if you desired, stop at the Basilian Fathers Museum and immerse yourself in a unique collection of Ukrainian liturgical texts from the 16th and 17th centuries. Failing that, why not stop for a moment beneath the world's largest sculpture of a garlic sausage? There are, to my knowledge, no contemporary accounts of Mundare, Alberta, that do not dwell on this sausage sculpture.

It's not only food that forms the thematic core of the roadside attraction, but bigness itself. Bigger than big. The very biggest. With the prevalent contempt for anything small, whatever is being erected on the side of the road is, by definition, big. It must, like the Trans-Canada Highway, be the biggest in the world. Consequently we have the world's largest axe, in Nackawic, New Brunswick; the world's largest piggy bank, in Coleman, Quebec; the world's largest illuminated fiddle, Sydney, Nova Scotia; the world's largest standing cuckoo clock, Kimberly, British Columbia; the world's largest hockey sticks in Dawson Creek, not to be confused with the world's largest hockey stick and puck at Duncan, British Columbia. Baseball lovers can treat themselves to "Suzie," the world's largest softball, in Chauvin, Alberta, population 378, a town in which more than thirty per cent of the homes are described as "moveable dwellings." The world's largest tree crusher can be found in Mackenzie, British Columbia. The world's largest painting on an easel is in Altona, Manitoba, and the world's largest purple martin house is in Neepawa, Manitoba, which also happens to be the Lily Capital of the World, the birthplace of Margaret Laurence, and the town where Canada's westernmost victim of the *Titanic*, Lewis Hickman, is buried. Actually, the body belongs not to Lewis Hickman but to his brother, Leonard. The mix-up was discovered an hour before the funeral, and the decision was made to seal the casket and carry on anyway. Neepawa is pleased to call Lewis Hickman one of its own, and why shouldn't it be?

Along with big comes Big Money. The modern road has long been associated with it, so it is perhaps not surprising that the world's largest nickel is to be found at Sudbury, Ontario. Sudbury is a friendly hard-rock town that witnessed its first female bicyclist in 1894 and its first boxing kangaroo in 1908, and whose early social milieu was presided over by a group of women known as "the Lonely Lasses of the Upper Classes," but there was a time not long ago when, if you went for a carriage ride to deliver a bouquet of roses to your sweet-heart, the roses would be wilted and black by the time you arrived. Sudbury's world's largest nickel is not to be mistaken, however, for the world's largest *wooden* nickel at Boiestown, New Brunswick. Echo Bay, Ontario, boasts the largest loonie. The largest toonie is to be found at Campbellford, Ontario. And on it goes. All of these over-sized coins offer a tribute to the belief—the bald hope—that the Canadian road is the road to success. They revel in an all-Canadian homespun vulgarity, and they do so without shame.

One does not need to be a Freudian to speculate that this em-phasis on being the world's biggest is also a reflection of a deep national insecurity. Often, it seems the basis of that insecurity is a perpetual fear that the tourists just won't come. These monuments act as a type of spell to ensure that they do, a shamanistic tribute to the cargo cult of the highway.

The Canadian master of the roadside monument was Winston Atwood Bronnum, who died in 1991. Bronnum, who quit school at grade three, was self-taught and worked out of a studio he called An-

imaland, located near the Timber-
line Motor Inn and Restaurant in
Sussex, New Brunswick. His work
has made him overwhelmingly
Canada's most viewed sculptor,
and arguably one of our most suc-

cessful artists. He has left behind him a legacy of oversized roadside
monuments, including the Shediac lobster, which, according to the
town of Shediac, brings in half a million tourists a year.

The curious legacy of Winston Bronnum includes just about
anything that is big—very big—in New Brunswick. His rare venture outside of that province gave the town of St. Thomas its legendary Jumbo sculpture, rearing up over the highway like an
enraged mammoth. One senses that perhaps Winston Bronnum
had a sharper understanding of what he was doing as an artist
than was initially suspected and that his "community monuments," as they have been called, are not as innocent as the roadside monument is meant to be. Consider *Broken Down Racehorse
(Blowhard)*, which stands outside the Timberland Motor Inn; this
gigantic starving animal is as stark a depiction of greed and in-
sensitivity as one is likely to find on the highway.

With the hostelry's dismal tourist information sign calling out
plaintively in the background, the viewer senses that whatever is
going on here, it isn't about the triumph of the road.

=╪═

In many ways the road is changing the landscape, not just with
roadside attractions and the innumerable yards of rock getting

carved from the hillsides, but with a new type of architecture as well. The appearance of the gas station in Canada, the first of which showed up in downtown Vancouver in 1907 and delivered gasoline through a garden hose, is the most recognizable. The gas station precipitated the disappearance of the blacksmith's shed in much the same way that the video store ushered in the disappearance of the local used book store. The gas station, however, has since become so recognizable as to be invisible. In their journey across the entire length of Canada, neither the Monsarrats nor the McCourts seemingly ever stopped at one, or if they did make no mention of it. The gas station has become so commonplace as to be unseen, a sort of poor and shameful relative whose invariably filthy bathrooms for some unfathomable reason require a key to get into, and not just any key, but one that dangles from a yardstick.

The cultural and architectural merit of such structures is given the most grudging status. The old faux chateau–style Joy Oil gas stations, most of which are gone now, represented a whimsical attempt to impose a type of gingerbread fantasy on the decidedly dirty business of burning fossil fuels. The last two standing examples of the Joy Oil stations have been declared historically significant and now sit on the north side of the Lakeshore in Toronto, draped in a pitiful tarp. They have been left literally on the side of the road and have been there for years, the rain pouring in through holes in the tarp. Despite the good intentions, they are not about to get enshrined in history any time soon. No one, it seems, has time.[1]

---

[1] In fact, time has been found. By this book's deadline, the station had been picked up from the north side of the Lakeshore and deposited on the south side of the Lakeshore, where the renovations are now taking place.

Once eccentric, personal and amusing, a great deal of roadside architecture, from the gas station to the motel to the strip mall, has succumbed to a standard design.

Along with the Lord of the Fries chip wagon, the Burger Bus, and the Bite Me Bait shop, the motel is another architectural space generated by the highway. A hybrid contraction of the words *motor* and *hotel*, the motel represents not only a new word created by the road, but a new state of confusion where home is a fleeting proposition that lasts typically no longer than a night and where the people who live in it are not entirely trustworthy.

Vance's Motor Inn is located in Spanish, Ontario, on the north side of the Trans-Canada as it parallels the North Channel, a leisurely, pastoral stretch of highway on the mainland above Manitoulin Island. Here the highway follows the migration of the Ojibwa west from the St. Lawrence as they followed the white megis shell to the mysterious place where food grows on water— the wild rice of Lake Superior. Despite this being Canada's central migration myth, the literature left in each room of Vance's Motor Inn does not mention it, does not mention any aspect of history at all. Instead, it assures the visitor that management is committed to providing something called "a great guest experience," an experience enhanced by a wide range of channels on the TV and the sound of trucks that pass directly outside the room. The motels of the Trans-Canada are located so close to the highway that the traffic can make the floors and ceilings vibrate. One misplaced tug of the steering wheel, and a truck's in the room with you.

The guest experience at Vance's Motor Inn is further enhanced by a view of the eroding white train station that sits on the other side of the Trans-Canada.

The station was built by the Canadian Pacific Railway in 1960 and was junked twelve years later in a cost-cutting move. It is a fine piece of work in "the International style," elegant and architecturally intriguing. It has rotted somewhat. Everything to do with the railway in Spanish, Ontario, seems to have rotted away. One gets the sense that it was meant to rot away, as if the prospect of *lasting*, or occupying any significant amount of time on Earth, was something the railway men preferred not to have happen.

The only thing that seems to last here is the pavement covering the highway, and even that must be constantly replenished, or "rehabilitated," as the engineers intriguingly put it, as though the road itself were a juvenile delinquent. The highway muscles its way through the very centre of town, cleaves it in half, and leaves everything in its wake sagging and demoralized. Each passing vehicle can serve as a reminder that people are going somewhere else. A traffic light hangs suspended over the highway in the middle of town: a timid yellow light that lacks the confidence to make people stop, or even to *request* that they stop, suggesting only that they might consider slowing down. Children who cross the street here cross the longest highway in the world, and they do so without protection of a traffic light. Town council urges them to walk their bicycles across this street. Theoretically, a crossing guard is provided Monday to Friday for approximately three hours each day. Parents are urged to wait for the crossing guard to be on duty before allowing their kids out of the house. Everything, including childhood, is pushed to the side by the physical reality of the road, the need for other people to go somewhere else.

Down the way from Vance's is a chip stand, another architectural achievement engendered by the highway. Nailed to it is an advertisement for Farquhar's Ice Cream, "made the old-fashioned way." In that heartbreaking phrase is sounded the betrayal of the railway for which this town was built, followed by the failure of the highway to play its much vaunted "vital role in the nation's economy." Even the future seems to have already failed somehow. "The old-fashioned way," that steadfast belief that things were better back then, before now, when we were young and before people sped through our lives at high speed behind tinted windows, has been left behind by the Trans-Canada. The old-fashioned way has become a road sign, and despite the rhetoric of the road, it does not take us back to those glorious days when the chickens walked around already cooked and the fish were impossible to keep off the hook. Increasingly, the highway takes us to a commercialized facsimile, a place called "Ye Olde Fashioned Way," in quotation marks.

Mounted next to the ad is another sign, this one for the Gateway Hot Dog. Presumably this particular hot dog is one that will open up the entire country to whoever eats it. It goes without saying that the Gateway Hot Dog is also a twelve-inch. The "12 inch" part has been added on later, hand-painted, in the touching confidence that the new and modernized traveller can no longer be persuaded to stop for a regular hot dog—it must be twelve inches to clinch the deal. There is no longer any "small," only "large, extra large, and jumbo large." Whether this hot dog is made the old-fashioned way is not stated. Perhaps it's a modern hot dog, or even a postmodern hot dog. Either way, it seems to be lost in the confusion of what the highway is supposed to be.

The black surface continues to roll on beneath these claims of hot dog and ice cream superiority. In defiance of town council, kids totter expertly back and forth across the highway on their bicycles, with no hands, their little sisters standing up on the bolts of the rear axle. And they do so in relative safety. Despite being the longest national highway in the world, the Trans-Canada is often completely empty, like a stage before showtime, or like the main street of any small town—this town, for example. There are moments when it appears no different from the way these lonely northern roads used to be: remote, destitute of travellers. Such destitution once prompted a gas station owner near English River to boast that at least fifty per cent of the cars that passed by his station would stop for gasoline, and that on very good days, "both of them would." It's an endearing truth about the Trans-Canada Highway that it occasionally resembles an old cart trail with barely enough room for two vehicles to pass side by side. It still seems as though it is possible to stop here, wait for an elderly woman's hen to lay eggs, and then give her a ride into town, the old-fashioned way.

Back in Vance's Motor Inn, the TV is on. The kids refuse to go to sleep and are bouncing up and down on the bed. They have never slept in a motel before and seem to view it as a type of indoor campsite. The trucks are ball-jacking their way east and west, but the drivers know better than to use their Jake brakes; there are signs that sternly warn them not to. Somewhere nearby, a white-throated sparrow is singing invisibly from a tree. The point between motion and stillness is here in this room. There is nothing more glorious than being in this room, and in many ways it is the road's proudest achievement to bring us here to Spanish, or Germanicus, or Inverhuron. To be everywhere and nowhere at the same time. The highway has accomplished it. Vance's Motor Inn has accomplished it. A small sticker attached to the window fronting the highway informs me that should I or anyone else in my family steal anything from this room, we will receive "life imprisonment." This unsettling statement is followed by the logo of the Ontario Provincial Police. We don't trust you, it says, you're a stranger, a mere traveller on the road, subjected to all the suspicion afforded the stranger. But we want your money.

=|=

At one time in early Canada, road signs and signposts were considered so important that to remove or tamper with them could result in a flogging. Now it seems a rite of passage to, at the very least, carve bullet holes in them. Or steal them. One of the stated reasons the city of Peterborough wanted to remove all road signs urging motorists to be on the lookout for crossing turtles was concern that the signs might be stolen. The other, perhaps more weighty concern, was that the signs didn't appear in the *Ontario Traffic Manual*. After being publicly embarrassed for attempting to get rid of the signs, not only by school kids but also by David Suzuki and author Yann Martel, council backed down, allowed the signs to stand, and began looking at finding a way to get the turtle signs included in the *Ontario Traffic Manual*. The support of Suzuki and Martel demonstrates that even writers themselves may have a minor role to play when it comes to writing the book of the road. As to the problem of theft, a thirteen-year-old student proposed to council that they coat the back of the signs with grease. The boy explained with some savvy that no one wants anything that dirty in the back seat of their car.

In the dreamy, vacuum-sealed comfort of today's automobile, with Mozart on the satellite radio, the kids watching DVDs from a portable or a built-in monitor, and a cell phone pressed to the driver's ear, the importance of the road sign increases. Yet amid the wash of onboard media distractions, combined with the massive, numbing quantity of signs, it is not clear just how much mental bandwidth we have left to absorb them. And there is a great deal to absorb. On one level, the book of the road is a large and complex instructional manual, informing us of how far we have yet to travel to reach South Porcupine or how fast we are legally allowed to go. A number of these signs are put up simply because it is someone's job to do so, or to at least do *something*: for example, "Wider vehicles take up more space." How carefully can the modern driver be expected to mull that one over? As of yet, there is no sign that states, "Smaller vehicles take up less space."

Less persnickety than signs of instruction and warning are signs of straightforward direction. When Thomas Wilby crossed an essentially signless Canada in 1912, he was amazed by the direction-finding abilities of a local school superintendent. The man, over time, had developed his own method of finding his way while driving. It's "dead easy with these sectional roads," he said. He went on to explain how the land was surveyed into quadrilateral townships, how each township contained thirty-six sections of 640 acres, and that a road allowance of one chain width ran north and south between each section and east and west between every alternate section, making a network of roads crossing at right angles. Using these basics, he was able to count ten miles from the last schoolhouse and thus locate himself. As far as Wilby was concerned the man might as well have said, "keep straight fifteen hundred miles and turn right to the south pole."

The Canadian Shield in particular is fertile ground for a different kind of sign: the spray-painted or hand-painted signs that appear unfailingly on rock that is so old it predates life on this planet, and unfailing offer a confession of love: "Ted loves Veronica always." *Ted loves Veronica always* is the basic love poem of the road, indicating that love is transportable and common, and linked somehow to movement. It is something that happens between Ted and Veronica; it is something that happens to all of us. The names change, but the sentiment doesn't. Hand- or spray-painted in black, red, or white, these messages represent the unofficial book of the road.

Provincial highway crews are sent out to erase this graffiti on a priority basis. Graffiti deemed to be offensive is removed first, but all of it, eventually, is to be deleted. These highway crews are the censors of the road, in charge of deciding whose love will survive and whose will be obliterated by a rectangle of grey paint. They don't understand, or care, that the world's longest road is a conduit of language. They know that bookmobiles, trucks laden with books, are moving across the land, from one remote northern library to another, that because of the highway it is now possible to read Seamus Heaney's translation of *Beowulf* in Nairn Centre, Ontario, and in Labrador City. But they don't accept that the exuberant and unofficial expressions of love that we paint on the rocks are born of the road itself. They are our *Beowulf*. They re-

call a day when the word was not a commodity to be sold, re-
viewed, anointed with a literary prize, and then finessed into a
movie. These painted messages belong to us. Their purpose is not
to sell anything. Instead, they are the raised middle finger to the
corporatization of the highway, and even the corporatization of
the written word. They bring in no tourist dollars; they pay no
monthly rental fees for the prime roadside space they occupy.
They are the only means we have to write our stories in the book
of the road, in particular the shortest of poems, which is, and always has been, our name—Ernie Kyle, NFLD, writ large on the oldest rock in the world.

These writings represent a non-Native form of rock art: roadside pictograms of no interest to the anthropologist or the cultural
agencies that seek to document, preserve, and explain the ancient
Aboriginal forms that adorn the rocks of Canada. They are seen, if
anything, as defacements and graffiti, the culture of the common
folk, and, even worse, the culture of the common folk who are not
long dead and shrouded in mystery.

But the road doesn't complain. It waits patiently for a time to
come when these hand-painted road signs are treated with the
same reverence reserved for pictograms at Agawa Rock. In the vast
compass of Lake Superior Provincial Park, these old, obscure, and
unfathomable drawings are offered to the public as a roadside cultural resource. Parking lots have been provided so that we might
drive up close to them. The parking lots are lined with carefully re-
searched and culturally sensitive signage to ensure that no one is
offended and that the pictograms' deep background can be ap-
preciated, even though, in truth, like the inukshuk, we don't know
the faintest thing about them, certainly not what they mean, or

even who put them there, or when. Should researchers eventually crack this lost code of squiggly lines and humanoid figures, they may determine that those power lines radiating from the head of a rabbit-eared man, those triangles painted in ochre and congealed with sturgeon oil, are singing into the endless north, "Ted loves Veronica always."

The road, like the rock surface that routinely surrounds it, is accessible to the common folk, and as such it presents a way around the official gatekeepers who try to keep us out: those editors who reject our manuscripts, the galleries that refuse to mount our paintings or show our fabulous sculptures. On the road, it is possible to give them the finger, or at least the thumb. The road becomes a gallery and even our means of advertising. Anyone driving through central Canada during the last few years will have encountered the billboard advertisement for the novel *The Minnow Trap*. Out here on the Trans-Canada, where Foucault is a guy who sells gas and performs small-engine repairs, authors do not stand on ceremony. They simply write a book, rent billboard space all along the highway, and arrange to have their books sold at coffee stops and at any place where you can still buy a dozen dew worms for under four dollars. They give readings at Tim Hortons, donating a portion of the proceeds of each book to charity. The fact that *The Minnow Trap* has been enthusiastically described as "the worst piece of pulp ever committed to paper" takes nothing away from the achievement. *The Minnow Trap*, for a while, towered over the Canadian Shield. Lately, those billboards have begun to peel and the whole enterprise is beginning to look a little dilapidated and even shabby. But for a brief period, its author literally took the high road and turned the tables on the Canadian publishing industry. He used the world's longest highway to find an alternative route to the reader, one that bypassed the sealed glass towers of downtown Toronto publishers. And he used the road to do it. He wrote and privately printed a novel. He plastered the Trans-Canada with advertisements for his bestseller ("quadruple bestseller," in his words—New York was knocking, or so he said, but he wasn't biting, at least not yet). He went from doughnut shop to gas station, where, eagerly and dramatically, he read aloud such sentences as, "Moaning sounds started coming out from various aliens." He demonstrated that the Canadian Road is still the people's road and that on its massive shoulders a Blind River businessman can turn himself into literary star, or at least a player.

The lessons have not gone unnoticed. Now these remote highways of blasted rock sport another billboard. Another staggering work is about to turn the world upside down. Billboards for another privately printed novel are making countless highway drivers scratch their head. Compared to *The Minnow Trap*, *The Converging* (Canada $13.99) is a literary masterpiece. ("Only by exposing the true face of evil can he protect the woman he loves and survive the horror of *The Converging*.") In the author bio, we learn that the author is married to Louise and that, together, they want us to "embrace compassionate living by being kind to the earth and its creatures." Similarly, the author of *The Minnow Trap* announces that he's married to Shirley. Brian and Shirley, George and Louise. Good people, solid people: women who tolerate and even encourage the idiosyncrasies of their husbands; men who know in their hearts that only by exposing the true face of evil can they protect the women they love. They have written massive, ponderous books, paid great sums of money to let the drivers of

Canada know about them, all in an effort to say one thing, the essential message of the road:

Ted loves Veronica always

STREET PEOPLE

The bus trip from Toronto to Vancouver is 4,374 kilometres and involves nearly takes three days and two nights of driving alongside trees, rock, and water, over prairies, up the white peaks of the Rocky Mountains, and finally down the long grades to the Pacific Ocean at Vancouver. The switchback on these grades can leave a bus driver's legs sore and strained from the constant braking required to keep the vehicle from going over the side. The carrier west is Greyhound Canada or its sister line, Grey Goose, whose coaches also often run Native passengers north to where the roads come to an end, usually at remote reserves that bear such beautiful and impossible names as God's Lake Narrows.

It's an exhausting ride that pounds the body into a rubbery

mass, and it's most typically taken by the young or the very old, those who do not own a car, those who can't afford to fly, or those who, by nature, need to feel the ground underneath them. A tinny percussive knock emanating from a dozen sets of headphones fills the interior of the bus, as does the gurgling of an ecstatic child. Young men stare out the windows; teenage mothers cradle remarkably compliant babies. Very old Cree or Ojibwa women are accompanied partway by their daughters or granddaughters, who get off somewhere along the highway, nowhere really, after deep, concerned embraces, leaving the old woman to brave the rest of the journey in silence and on her own. It isn't unusual for the buses to have numerous television screens hanging from the ceiling. The bus itself stands remarkably tall. All the long-distance buses stand tall for the simple reason that they are now designed to transport cargo in the luggage bins. As a moneymaker, the passengers come second.

Boarding this vehicle means standing in the blue fumes and grey interior of the Toronto Coach Terminal, an immense concrete bunker exuding the sadness that, according to Jack Kerouac, is unique to bus stations. It is the sadness of departure, of leaving, of motion without luxury, and of the bus station itself, an architectural reminder that you are, in this moment, homeless. Despite that, the very greyness of the place itself thrums with the possibility of travel: the deep, almost sexual appeal of transporting yourself somewhere else, the sheer nervousness of taking to the road and of earning the road, mile by mile. It also means listening to what is surely the geographically longest sentence in the English language as it crackles over the public address system in the terminal. The sentence is spoken by a woman, and she begins sedately enough: "This is the last call for Greyhound Coach number six-fifty-eight leaving the Bay Street Terminal, gate number five, from Toronto to Vancouver via Parry Sound, Sudbury, Espanola, Spanish, Serpent River, Thessalon Junction, Bruce Mines, Sault Ste Marie, Heyden, Pancake Bay, Wawa . . ." This litany of names is like the names of lovers we have known and parted from. Before she has finished, she will have covered 4374 kilometres, proceeding almost due north, then north by northwest, mingling together place names in at least five different languages: Algonquian, English, French, Sioux, and even Spanish. Now these names come together like the roll call of a large family that has grown comfortable with itself and its differences: "White River, Marathon, Terrace Bay, Schreiber, Nipigon, Red Rock Junction, Dorion, Thunder Bay, Upsala, Ignace, Wabigoon, Kenora . . ."

At this point, her voice sheds some of its terminal greyness, as if it has just dawned on her how much energy she will need to breast the Canadian Shield. Somehow, without taking a breath, she bursts out of Ontario, accelerating across Prairie straightaways—"Winnipeg, Elie Junction, Portage la Prairie, MacGregor, Austin, Carberry, Brandon, Virden, Elkhorn, Moosomin"—until it seems there are too many names, too many places for anyone to pass through in a single life, too many lovers—"Wapella, Whitewood, Sintaluta, Indian Head, Regina, Moose Jaw, Swift Current . . ."—a litany of unlikely places, beads strung together on a single unlikely wire: "Gull Lake, Maple Creek, Medicine Hat, Bassano, Calgary, Canmore, Banff, Lake Louise, Golden, Rogers Pass, Revelstoke, Sicamous, Salmon Arm, Sorrento, Chase, Kamloops, Merritt, Hope . . ." The sentence ends, with a thud, in Vancouver and is followed by two limp words: "Last call."

Smoking hasn't been allowed on a Greyhound bus for many years, and posted regulations insist it's against the law to strike up a conversation with the bus driver, even though bus drivers often rank among the chattiest people you will ever meet. It is also against the law to transport caribou heads, spiders, and stuffed game animals.

Despite the warnings, the young man seated beside me is determinedly concealing a live eastern slant-eyed turtle on an epic voyage from Mississauga, Ontario, to Vancouver, British Columbia. The turtle is hidden away in a small cardboard box with a towel placed over the top of it. The young man is a seasoned veteran of these transcontinental rides; his name is Ron and he has crossed the country six times by bus. "Six times," he says, defying me, or anyone, to outdo him. He considers himself to be one of the great Canadian crossers, and it feels impolite to remind him that, nearly a century ago, Pauline Johnson crossed this same country nineteen times, riding on trains that wrecked, sailing in ships that sank, and sleeping in hotels that burned down on her. Nineteen times across the Rockies. An odd number means that you never come home. It means you die somewhere else.

Periodically the young man removes the towel from the top of the box and peers in at his turtle. This time, his turtle is coming with him, and he frequently folds back the towel to cast loving and tender looks down into the box. Eventually, and with great aplomb, he takes out a book, a Stephen King novel, and holds it in front of him.

"I don't know how to read," he whispers.

"No?"

"No. I'm illiterate. It makes me feel important when I got a

book open. It makes people think I can read. Right?" There is
something desperate in his voice, as if in this very moment it has
dawned on him how isolated he is.

"Right."

He seems satisfied by this answer, and we don't talk again. Just
a boy and his turtle, taking the road to somewhere else.

In the last of the twilight of day two, I find myself shoulder to
shoulder with a hulking overaged junior hockey player from the
Soo Greyhounds. He has just signed a pro contract with the Tampa
Bay Lightning and he's going home to Winnipeg and he's happy,
polite, and animated, like a soldier. We talk hockey: the big hit-
ters, who's the hardest to clear out from the front of the net, and
so on. Suddenly, without provocation, he solemnly informs me
that the best-looking women in Canada live in Winnipeg. "There's
some real good ones there," he says, and when he disembarks at
the terminal, he heads off brusquely, with great determination, as
if to roust up a couple of them.

In the dark, black as obsidian now, I allow myself to engage in
the thrill of eavesdropping. Two elderly women are seated across
from me. Their age, their sex, the road itself has joined them into
a somewhat prickly intimacy, and they talk about the hardships of
long bus rides, the hardships of womanhood and age, and of loneliness. "It must be terrible having to eat alone," says one softly.
The other one snorts. "Ha," she says. She wants nothing to do with
pity or sympathy, or the terribleness of things. She's been down
that road before, many times. "I been doing it for forty years. I'm
used to it."

Later, I am plunked down next to a hard-knitting, fast-talking
woman from Winnipeg. Without prompting, she begins to lament

the fate of her no-good son, who, in her opinion, ought to be in hospital on account of a severe beating he received in a bar fight. "You watch," she says. "He'll get himself killed one night. He will. Someone'll cut him open with a broken beer bottle. I know all about that because that's how my husband died. It was one of those Frenchmen who did it, half-breed too. Jabbed him in the back end with a broken beer bottle, five days later he died of infection." She puts down her knitting for a moment and gives me a solemn stare. "I'm no racist," she says, "but when it comes to fighting with a broken beer bottle, those half-breed Frenchies, they're the worst."

I find myself taking her word for it. The wisdom we acquire on the road.

=||=

Whether we go by bus, by car, or any type of vehicle whatsoever, it seems that the foremost function of the road is to create us. It facilitates the great community of "us" in all our itinerantness, in all our unlikely attempts to put down stakes in towns that are too small to contain their names, or in cities too big to know our neighbours. We encounter it in the fleeting timelessness of motion: *us*. We're there every time the car stops. We are the first person we meet on the road.

We are waiting at the end of a southbound turn off the Trans-Canada at Neys, Ontario, which is not a town at all but a name, a crossroad, a camp and trailer park, a gas station, and a welcome general store that sells trout lures the size of a human hand, alongside tins of canned meat, beer, and mosquito repellent. Lots of mosquito repellent. To take the crossroad heading south off the highway here is to drive down the twisting road beneath the red sumac trees with their lumpy red fruits that burn as bright as votive candles. A short distance in front of the car, a skinny wolf limps across the road. Its tongue is lolling and it pays us no mind at all. Two cubs prance behind, but the wolf herself looks alarmingly like an exhausted and overworked parent who's not getting enough sleep. Then the park gates, Neys Provincial Park, where we are processed by a fresh-faced, astonishingly healthy-looking girl in a park regulation brown uniform, wearing a name tag that reads "Ashley." It seems that all the healthy young women who work the gatehouses of provincial parks wear name tags that say Ashley.

These parks are the jewels of the Trans-Canada Highway and, like the motel, the shopping mall, and the highway billboard, they were conceived and implemented in tandem with the great road. The parks are spaced in such a way that they allow us to start at one end of the country and camp our way to the other without ever once touching down in a hotel or motel, or any other place that offers a "great guest experience." At one time, it was presumed that this was what Canadians would do, camp like the old voyageurs, eating our bannock, singing songs, telling entertaining lies to one another. American campers adore them for their spaciousness, their privacy, their scenery, and because they can turn their children over to a twenty-year-old socialist named Ashley who will take them out on a nature walk and return them safely and on the dot two hours later while their parents sit around the campsite with their feet up, telling entertaining lies.

The brightest of these jewels is Neys, a name without a place really, a contraction of Doheney's, from the old railway-building days when nearly every non-Native place name in Canada derived from some engineer associated with the building of the railway. During World War II, it was a prisoner of war camp: hardened Nazis were kept here, fighter pilots mostly, "the Blacks," they were called, in deference to their extreme Nazi beliefs. Now it's a provincial park, the bears pass through it at will, and the lakefront, it is fair to say, is the most stunning freshwater beach in the world, framed by ancient mountains. The sky is scored by the regular passing of eagles and immense osprey that hurtle themselves straight down, striking the surface of the water several yards away from where you swim, sending up an enormous plume of water, and a moment later emerging clutching a fish the size of your arm, so big, in fact, that the bird must circle downwind before getting up enough speed to mount the sky and go upriver.

A man from Winnipeg is seated on a camp chair on the sand. He's a veteran of this place, and as I pass along the beach in front of him, he makes the universal gesture for "Keep your mouth shut," his forefinger intersecting his lips. He shakes his head. "Look, pal," he's saying. "Let's keep this place secret. Let's not spill the beans. Just you and me, buddy."

Of course I agree, but the secret is out. It was outed by the road that made this place entirely accessible, and it has been outed by me in my inability to shut up about it. Probably because of its sheer *nowhereness*, situated as it is a few miles off Dead Horse Creek, people still don't stop here much, and this unites the two of us. We begin to talk, and I sense his warmth, his goodwill. He's the sort of man who pulls off the highway to help you change a flat tire. He's a Westerner. He has a Westerner's openness and the Westerner's fanatical love of football, even high school football, and he's here for a vacation. He wouldn't think of going anywhere else.

We talk. Mostly, he talks. He passes on his cargo of stories. At the age of fourteen, while running downfield to catch a football, he tripped, head over heels, over a black bear. "I went one way," he says, "it went the other." Five years ago, at the age of fifty-seven, he was struck by lightning while emerging from the Red River. All that he remembers is finding himself on the bank, on his hands and knees, vomiting. "Did it change you?" I ask, wondering if he emerged with a head full of luminescent blue light or the sudden ability to play Chopin on the piano. He gives the question serious thought. "Yeah, it did," he says finally. "It made me scared shitless of getting hit by lightning."

The Nazis who were held here were very young and very fit men, and when they escaped, they were sometimes captured on the nearest dance floor. I find myself wondering if the military police let the song come to an end before they hauled them back to the camp. The Japanese were interned here as well. I learn this from a friendly woman named Rosemarie.

Rosemarie is, or was, the sole curator, operator, and fundraiser for the nearby Marathon District Museum. The museum is a small, distinct structure, formerly a library, then a youth drop-in centre, which explains the blue-tinged punctures in the low ceiling, left over from excited pool players who jabbed their cues in the air. When I first met Rosemarie, she was sitting inside the museum in the dark. A $5,000 operating grant had been denied, and the Marathon District Museum didn't have enough money for electricity. Even if the place were entirely in the dark, if you knocked, there was a very good chance that Rosemarie would turn on the lights and be willing to talk to you.

The museum is in possession of the box scores of about every Marathon Mercs hockey game dating back to 1946. These are the vital statistics of history: who scored the goal, the assist, and even the second assist. Rosemarie is, by default, the keeper of these statistics.

She is also a talker, and her stories pass as swiftly as the trucks on the highway. Many of these stories are told at the expense of our U.S. neighbours and are suspect variations on the border checkpoint story, the one that sees an American tourist showing up in August with skis attached to his roof rack. These tales don't seem particularly ill-motivated. If anything, they are inevitable, reminding us that a function of the highway is to bring these folks here in the hope that we might be able to cash in on them, or at least get a chuckle out of them. One gets the sense that, like God himself, if ill-informed American tourists didn't exist, we would have to invent them. You meet such people all the time on the Canadian road: the large, friendly man with Arizona licence plates on his vehicle who points to Lake Superior and says, "What's the name of that ocean and when's the best time to see the whales?" These stories are told straight up by young park employees, with no suggestion that this bluff Arizonian is perhaps pulling their leg or turning the table on their own expectations of American tourists.

It isn't the sort of question that an American tourist, or anyone else, for that matter, wants to ask Rosemarie. Rosemarie is a large, frank woman who has a way with language. She refers to severe clinical depression as "losing your hee haw." She is one of the few people left in Canada who can authentically call a moose a "swamp donkey." She has the endearing and geographically rare accent that pronounces *southern* as *sowthern*. Her husband is known as Bingo. Perhaps he has another name, but if he does, no one seems to know what it is. Not even him. You get the sense one day it will be carved on his tombstone: "Here, under the B, lies Bingo."

In a restaurant, an innocent American tourist has made the mistake of eavesdropping on Rosemarie's conversation about the art of smoking fish. "Excuse me," he says politely. He has found himself face to face with the wisdom of the Canadian Northerner, and he wants in on it. "I heard you talking about how to smoke fish and I want to know how to do it, I mean the right way. You hear so much bullshit."

"You sure do," agrees Rosemarie with perhaps too much enthusiasm, and her companions are already turning away, embarrassed for the man, embarrassed for themselves. Rosemarie starts in with all the congenial authority of a family doctor on a radio phone-in show. "Okay, this is how you do it. First you put the fish on its side and you gut it, you take your filleting knife and cut down right behind the gill until you reach the spine—"

"Wait a sec," says the man. "I want to write this down," and he retreats to his table to rummage in a satchel. By now, Rosemarie's companions are sunk in gloom. One of them has his head in his hands. The man returns.

"Okay," says Rosemarie, "you reach the spine with the filleting knife and you stop there. That's the trick—you got to stop right there." Rosemarie pauses long enough for him to catch up. "Once you've done that, you take off the dorsal fin. Slip the blade just beneath the dorsal fin, slide down toward the tail. Okay?" The man nods. "Good," she says. "So after you hack off the dorsal fin, you put that to one side, then you take your tobacco and roll it into the centre of the fish and then you sew it up. Then take your lighter, eh? A Zippo—got to be a Zippo. Hold the flame to the tail.

Once that catches, you suck real hard on the mouth.

"And that," says Rosemarie, "is how you smoke a fish."

It is common here, at latitude 55, for the roads to be impassable with snow. In fact, the Trans-Canada Highway, especially on the Superior shore, is punctuated at regular intervals by a large circular turnouts carved into the four-billion-year-old rock that frames the road. These structures allow the snowplows space to turn around. When the roads are shut due to snow, people tend to stay indoors. Doctors make house calls on snowmobiles. At dinnertime, people order in pizza, which also comes by snowmobile—not, perhaps, what Joseph Armand Bombardier had in mind when in 1960 he was granted a Canadian patent to produce an endless-track snow machine. Local people who own a snowmobile are pressed into service and can pick up a few dollars with impromptu freelance work. Strangely, tips for a pizza delivered during a blinding snowstorm from the back of a snowmobile are noticeably less generous than for a pizza delivered by car on a bright summer day. The logic is perplexing: it says something about hardship and bad weather, how all of us are required to pay for it.

Regardless of the weather, a number of extraordinary crashes take place on the nearby Trans-Canada, and Rosemarie is a walking archive of nearly all of them. In our talks, she provides me with some rare information about a not-very-noble road tradition, one that duplicates the old "wreckers" of the great sailing era, when savage villagers ruthlessly ransacked the contents of wrecked vessels that washed against their shores, murdering the survivors in the process. These are kinder, modern-day road wreckers who pilfer the cargo of crashed transport trucks, sneaking in at night to take advantage of the misfortune of others. To their credit, they don't murder the drivers. Rosemarie recalls the contents of a toppled-over ice cream truck that stayed frozen long enough to end up in people's freezers. This accident was immediately followed by a cheese truck that caught on fire. "For a week," says Rosemarie, "we had fondue."

In the end, this may be the one great financial payload that the Highway of Hope finally delivers: a few scattered items stolen furtively from the ditch while a broken truck lies on its side. There is a deep and sophisticated Canadian morality at play here. I hear it in Rosemarie's story, as I've heard it in other stories told by fast-talking old-timers who have described train wrecks to me, and how penniless farmers came out at night to take away the spilled wheat or the grain. Almost without exception, they were betrayed. That wheat turns out to be fall wheat, which is planted but doesn't grow, so entire fields have been wasted for a season. Those pints of ice cream, that cottage cheese hoarded off the highway? They're curdled—gone bad. You end up having to throw them out. Even those priceless sides of beef stealthily tossed onto the back of an ATV or a snowmobile, on closer inspection with a flashlight, reveal a mocking disclaimer stenciled in blue: Tainted meat—for animal consumption only.

So ends Rosemarie's story, with a knowing laugh. The road is a stage on which moral certitudes assert themselves. In this case, the road insists upon what everybody understands: that we'll never get anything for free. Not in this country. Even to want something for free is suspect, almost evil. Rosemarie laughs out loud at the conclusion of this story. She is laughing at the people themselves, at herself, for being so foolish as to forget that.

=⌐

West of here, at twilight, on a dark, lapping shore in Fort Frances, I stand next to a young man who is doing exactly that: getting something for free. In this case, it's fish. The man is leaning against his truck effortlessly pulling out one walleye after another. "Got one," he says, matter-of-factly, his rod bending like a question mark as he swings a foot-long walleye out of the water. I explain that we've just spent thirty dollars on a fish like that in a local restaurant. He nods. "Yeah, but sometimes it's worth it to have someone else clean up the dishes, right?" In the time it takes to say this, he pulls out another walleye and tosses it on the grass, where it flops next to the first one.

While we stand there, a train bursts out of the trees, a freight laden with chemical containers, crossing a small trestle bridge that spans the river and joins Canada to the United States of America. "Our good old patriotic brothers," he says vaguely to the air, and snaps a third foot-long walleye from the water. This one he tosses back as he grins at me. "I don't call this fishing, really. Just gettin' away from the wife and the kids for a while." There is something disarming in this weary ball-and-chain performance coming from a man who is barely twenty years old and looks considerably younger. His truck is the size of a tank and seems to contain within it all the crushing responsibility he bears: the young children, the young wife, the new mortgage, the shift work, the heavy burden of paternal cynicism. The road is all around him, it extends in any possible direction he could want, but it hasn't led to any freedom that he can perceive. It has led instead to an almost compulsory expression of dissatisfaction. Somehow it doesn't seem authentic coming from this youngster, but rather like an act appropriated from an older relative or an older peer group of men. "There's a school here," he points to the dark water just off shore. "I come here at night, for twenty minutes, to get away from, you know . . ."

"Yes," I say quickly, "I know."

He nods, pulls out another fish, and returns it.

There are many who maintain that the walleye is the finest-tasting fish on the planet, and there's something exhilarating about watching this fellow take out a fish that, except on rare occasions, can't be had for love or money in Paris or Toronto or New York. In Fort Frances, Ontario, however, the walleye are piling up at our feet like domestic responsibilities, until finally the young fisher has had enough. In the last five minutes, he has caught himself nine brilliant fish and returned five of them.

"The only thing," he says, pulling out one last blue beauty that he eyeballs and tosses back into the water, "is the bugs, eh?" It is true that for the last few minutes the bugs have been coming at us like kamikaze pilots, the moths and flies striking our bodies with such force that they fall, stunned, to the ground. Almost apologetically, the young man bids me goodnight, climbs into his massive truck, and is gone into the night.

=|=

The road is not just a space in which we talk, chatter, and reveal ourselves. It is also a very funny place, a place of wit, and on its back we transport our national sense of humour. In many cases, it's the actual stage where the humour is performed. The Tramore

Road is an old, storied cottagers' highway in Eastern Ontario. More often than not, it's devoid of traffic, but at one time, during the late 19th century, this road regularly took an army of teamsters and lumbermen up to the headwaters of the Bonnechere River to commence the annual log run. There are written descriptions of this road literally *black* with men and horses from top to bottom, twenty-fours a day.

It was on or near this road that a wit by the name of Paddy Garvey was reported to have travelled, lugging a cast-iron stove and leading behind him a pregnant sow on a rope. To Paddy's misfortune, this sow gave birth and poor Paddy was reduced to chasing newborn piglets around in the woods while carrying that bone-crushing cast-iron stove on his suffering back. Today, the modern Canadian would simply *put the stove down* before rounding up the piglets—the quintessentially Northern humour revealed in that anecdote would soon become nearly incomprehensible.

A new generation of men and women—writers, editors, critics—would hurry down a different road, fawning over Europe, longing for New York, and aping the styles of London in a desperate attempt to appear sophisticated. The pages of Canadian magazines would soon fill with their precious prose, and the age of indoor writing, even the age of indoor Canada, would begin. No longer would people tell the tale of Paddy Garvey who went "up the Karcajoo" carrying an iron stove on his back.

But before that happened, the wit of the Ottawa Valley was to get off one last ringing toast to Canadian humour. In a drunken stupor, staggering home along the Opeongo Line one night, Paddy Garvey was confronted by the village priest. "Drunk again, Paddy?" the priest demanded. To which the blithe Irishman answered, "Me too, Father, me too."

It is this wit that the road spreads from one end of the country to the other: a logic-defying, anti-grammatical outburst that at first sounds like plain stupidity but on closer inspection reveals a profound distrust of language, of common sense, and of nature. Nature, said the New York wit Fran Lebowitz, is what happens between the hotel and the taxi. This might apply well enough to the teeming streets of New York City, but on the Cariboo Trail, the Trans-Canada Highway, or the Opeongo Line, nature isn't a sidebar between two other stories; it *is* the story. Nature is what closes down the roads leading to the hotel and causes the taxi to skid out of control. Typically, those hotels are no great shakes to begin with, as indicated by a frank sign once posted in the lobby of the Stag Hotel in Golden City, Ontario: We know this hotel is on the bum. What about yourself?

This humour has never died. It lives on in a small public park in Massey, Ontario, on a spit of land where the Aux Sable River meets the Mississagi. An old but functioning outhouse stands humbly beneath a majestic tree.
On the side of it, painted in white and spelled not altogether correctly, are three words: *No assholes alowed.*

Given a chance, the road will take us into the authentic, all right. It's just that, once we get there, it might not look the way we thought it would.

Highway 22, westbound out of Esterhazy, Saskatchewan, a province, wrote Percy Gomery in 1922, "where the roads were so cruel and the people so kind." We are driving through the canola, brilliant yellow, a colour that appears too rich to be of this world. Well in front of the windshield lies that strange optical illusion of the paved Prairie highway: a pool of water, or so it seems, lying directly across the road a hundred yards ahead. And yet that hundred yards is never covered; that pool, that strange watery discoloration, recedes forever.

Off to the side, an old, abandoned drive-in movie screen rises out of the scrub between the fields. It leans ominously forward, like some once mighty giant reduced to decrepitude. But even in this state of abandonment, the drive-in calls up powerful memories: children in pajamas, spinning around on the painted tin carousel in front of the screen. Over top of them appear the vast faces of the silver screen. The darkness isn't full-on yet, and the images only brush the fabric like ghosts. The children don't care; they're rocking back and forth on plastic ducks mounted on fat spring coils, or they're clinging to the ever-turning carousel. In a few minutes, they're led away crying or carried limply to the back seat of the car and ushered into sleep. A man adjusts the single dial on the heavy steel speaker clamped to the inside of the window. His wife folds her legs and gets comfortable. The deep, booming voice of an American actor floods the interior of the car. The children sleep through nearly all of it, awakening only for a few confused moments in the press of cars at the end, when the screen has gone white and the vehicles assemble like corralled horses, trying to get out through two tightly packed exits. The speaker is handed back through the window to the attendant. The movie is over, the cars and the families inside them are driving home content and satiated.

Now, on Highway 22, it is only too obvious that a once familiar scene of family and community is gone. The surface of the screen is peeling off like dried skin. Nothing is playing here; nothing has played for years. The parking lot is grown over, and the screen juts up from it like a skeletal frame on which dreams were once projected. Not long ago, the road took us here, Canadians in American-made cars, to gather and watch American-made films. From the safety of plush interiors, we witnessed crimes that were more criminal than our own, jokes that were funnier, kisses that were longer and more passionate than Canadian kisses. At some point, in front of these fading screens, we made our first staggering contact with a lover's body, squirming, fiddling with zippers. There's a couple in the front seat, another couple in the back. The movie, from the beginning, was just a clever distraction designed to light up the night sky and pacify the parents. *The Exorcist, Ranch of the Nymphomaniac Girls,* old Vincent Price horror films in particular—all of them admirably suited the gropings that took place beneath the screen. The passion was so intense that after several moments of it, the interior of the car windows had fogged up. "Have I done this?" We're caught up in the wonder of ourselves and fall back into the car seat, into the warm body of the one we are with, infinitely pleased with who we are and the road that we're travelling.

Today, that road is behind us. The drive-in movie screen has peeled away in sheets, revealing the dull grey paint and nothing more. The screen stands decrepit, ignored in a bit of scrub land. No one stops here anymore. We are in constant motion, travelling across the land. Westward, always westward . . .

Highway 22, somewhere between Calgary and the foothills, heading toward a place called Bragg Creek, a quiet, rather toney town that bills itself as the Backyard Adventure Playground of Alberta. The road continues to turn the earth into a playground, but this one, being a Western playground, is an "adventure playground," which implies at least a slight whiff of danger. The road to town is swarming with furtive brown creatures, quick as squirrels but smaller, dashing across the highway. These would be the gophers that got caught up in the spokes of Thomas Wilby's Oldsmobile in 1912. As quick as they are, they're not quite quick enough, and I watch the car in front of me deliberately swerve out of its way to splatter them. The bland, commonplace thrill of causing death.

At Bragg Creek, off Highway 22 west out of Calgary, I am introduced to a hard-riding, hard-shooting gang of Western artists and writers with whom I am to reside for a week. One of them, a muscular, bearded cartoonist, keeps his paints and pastels in a steel munitions container, sharpens his pencil crayons with a large,

jagged bowie knife fastened to his hip, and drives around in a car on which is mounted a large-calibre machine gun made out of cardboard.

"So you're from the East," he says, not looking up from his sketchbook. "In the West, we have a saying for people

from the East. It goes, 'Fuck off.'" He later explains that, in his opinion, Canada should change its name—to Ontario. "Really, let's be
honest about it."

"If we're going to be honest, why not just call the whole country Fort McMurray?"

"Fort McMurray is a shithole," he says, and both of us laugh.

It is afternoon, and out the open window of the room where I'm
staying I hear the *hush-hushing* of traffic from the highway nearby—
the highway that has brought me here. For me, it's the end of the
road. Out on the grass below my window, I watch a eulogy taking
place. A group of colleagues form a circle in the grass, mourning
their deceased friend. A man, head bowed, reads a poem:

> *I have been driving   the streets*
> *   all day*
> *the pavement black*
> *   with   conversation coursing*
> *   between*
> *   tires   and itself*
> *the cars leave*
> *   ten thousand syllables*

He invokes the road to lament the death of a friend; it is where
the road will take us. There is one less rider on the highway, and we
are diminished for it. The community of ourselves is one smaller,
and because the vanished person is a poet, it means that our word
hoard has been made smaller too. Later, when I read the text of the

poem, with the drifting and erratic location of the phrases, I can't help but think, correctly or not, that this person was killed in a car accident or skidded off the road, like so many before.

Soon the service breaks up and the lawn empties. I lie down on the bed, exhausted after the long ride, and try to will myself to sleep by invoking an old dream of motion. Beneath my eyelids, the grey road rolls beneath me in the rain. The land is blurred with fog, everything is blurred, but the dream continues, a waking dream comprised of the unending desire to see what I have never seen before, to reach the foothills and, like Henry Kelsey before me, to make contact with the western Nawatayme Poets. It is a decent dream.

I'm still dreaming it when I fly home and witness the roads of Canada spread out beneath the plane like the veins of a living body. Then I'm back in the stationary comfort of my office. The computer grinds away. There, on that small windshield of my screen, I come across an item for sale: a vehicle, for which its owner has no more use. He has moved on. His road has taken a different route, even a different shape. A road has ended, and it strikes me that all these fabled roads that supposedly never end, they *do* end; it's just that they don't end where we expect them to, at the meeting place of land and ocean. Instead they end at a crossroads that we hardly ever see coming, the intersection between being young and being something else.

The item is in the classified section of *Quill & Quire*, and it states simply

Pink ambulance for sale cheap: gently used by
poet/performance artist Mingus Tourette.

ACKNOWLEDGEMENTS

Along the various roads I took to write this book, I was assisted by a capable assortment of wayfarers that included gas attendants, editors, book designers, librarians, short order cooks, brewers of strong coffee, and dedicated custodians of local history. I am massively indebted to all of them, as I am to my research assistant, navigator, co-driver, and wife, Deborah Clipperton. I would also like to thank my daughters for belting out their enthusiasms from their booster seats in the back, and for bringing song, cheer, and wit to this journey.

My thanks to Rosemarie Comeau and Tamby Fair of the Marathon District Historical Museum for their hospitality and assistance, to Matthew Harvey of the Ontario Ministry of Natural Resources, to Joelle Kovach, and to Percy Toop. Thanks to Gerald Kernerman and Leah Vosko for their support and for providing me with documents, resources, and sources that I would have otherwise missed. Jerry McGrath and Alan McMillan endured many hours of me going on about this project, and for that I am grateful.

My agent, Hilary McMahon, once again proved herself a skilled leader of any expedition, and my editor, Jane Warren, very capably and genially let me know when I was lost and offered many suggestions as to how I might be found. Many thanks are due to Key Porter Books for their support and also to the Ontario Arts Council, the Toronto Arts Council, and the Canada Council for the Arts. Thanks also to Mingus Tourette, Bob Stallworthy, Gail Sidonie Sobat, Spider Jones, and others for their support and inspiration. Finally, to all those fellow scribblers who post their thoughts, photos, and reminiscences on the great virtual highway, my deepest and sincerest thanks.

SELECTED REFERENCES

INTRODUCTION

Historical Committee, Public Safety Information Branch, *Footpaths to Freeways: The History of Ontario's Roads: Ontario's Bicentennial 1784–1984*. Toronto: Ontario Ministry of Transportation and Communications, 1984.

Edwin C. Guillet, *The Story of Canadian Roads*. Toronto: University of Toronto Press, 1967.

David W. Monaghan, *Canada's "New Main Street": The Trans-Canada Highway as Idea and Reality 1912-1956*. Ottawa: Canada Science and Technology Museum, 2002.

Valerie Knowles, *From Telegraph to Titan: The Life of William C. Van Horne*. Toronto: Dundurn, 2004.

Thomas Wilby, *A Motor Tour Through Canada*. London: John Lane, 1914.

CHAPTER ONE: WINDSHIELD TIME

Mingus Tourette, *Nunt*. Edmonton, AB: Zygote Publishing, 2004.

Beat Museum, www.beatmuseum.org/welch/LewWelch.html.

CHAPTER TWO:

FEET ON THE GROUND: THE ROADLESS ROAD

Henry Kelsey, introduction by John Warkentin, *The Kelsey Papers*.
Regina, SK: Canadian Plains Research Center, University of Regina,
1994.

Horatio Hale, ed., *The Iroquois Book of Rites*. Toronto: Coles, 1972.

Dennis F. Johnson, *York Boats of the Hudson's Bay Company: Canada's
Inland Armada*. Calgary, AB: Fifth House, 2006.

Peter Nabokov, *Indian Running: Native American History and Tradition*.
Santa Fe, NV: Ancient City Press, 1987.

CHAPTER THREE: BREAKING THE TRAIL

Donald E. Graves, ed., *Merry Hearts Make Light Days: The War of 1812
Journal of Lieutenant John Le Couteur, 104th Foot*. Ottawa: Carleton
University Press, 1993.

Edwin C. Guillet, *The Story of Canadian Roads*. Toronto: University of
Toronto Press, 1967.

Dennis F. Johnson, *York Boats of the Hudson's Bay Company: Canada's
Inland Armada*. Calgary, AB: Fifth House, 2006.

Marilyn G. Miller, *Straight Lines in Curved Space: Colonization Roads
in Eastern Canada*. Toronto: Ontario Ministry of Culture and
Recreation, 1978.

Barbara Huck et al., *Exploring the Fur Trade Routes of North America*,
2nd ed. Winnipeg, MA: Heartland Associates, 2002.

CHAPTER FOUR: UP THE CREEK WITHOUT A HORSE:
THE ARRIVAL OF THE "RUNNING STINKER"

"On the Right side of the Road." www.fhwa.dot.gov/infrastructure/
right.htm.

"Automobiles: The Early Days in NS."
www.littletechshoppe.com/ns1625/automobiles.html.

"George Foote Foss." www.townshipsheritage.com/Eng/Hist/FamousInv/
foss.html.

Marcel Granger, "Henry Seth Taylor Steam Buggy."
www.lino.com/~marcelg/boghe_an.htm.
The Oil Sport, Eh?, www.theoilspoteh.ca/trivia.htm.

CHAPTER FIVE: LITTLE DICTATORS
Thomas Wilby, *A Motor Tour Through Canada*. London: John Lane, 1914.
"Jack Haney's Diary." wolfe.vsb.ca/autotour/diary.htm.
"Doolittle, Dr. Perry E. Coast to Coast by Automobile."
http://empireclubfoundation.com.
"About CAA History." www.caaneo.on.ca.
Percy Gomery, *A Motor Scamper Cross Canada: A Human-Interest Narrative of a Pathfinding Journey from Montreal to Vancouver*. Toronto: Ryerson, 1922.
Pierre Radisson, *The Voyages of Pierre Esprit Radisson*. New York: Publication of the Prince Society, 1885.
Edward McCourt, *The Road Across Canada*. Toronto: Macmillan, 1965.
Ontario Motor League, *Road Book, 1959–1960*. Toronto: Ontario Motor League, 1959.
Nicholas Monsarrat, *Canada Coast to Coast*. London: Cassel and Company, 1955.
Susan Williams, *Colour Bar*. London: Allen Lane, 2006.

CHAPTER SIX: HIGHWAY TO THE MOUNTAINS
Janet Flanner, "Annals of Collaboration," Parts 1–3. *The New Yorker*, October 1945.
Jim Christy, *The Price of Power: A Biography of Charles Eugene Bedaux*. Toronto: Doubleday, 1984.
Pierre Berton, *The Remarkable Past: Tales from My Country and the Wild Frontier*. Toronto: McClelland & Stewart, 1995.
"Biography of Charles Eugene Bedaux."
www.managers-net/Biography/biograph3.html.

CHAPTER SEVEN: THE ROADS MOST TRAVELLED
Daniel Francis, *A Road for Canada: The Illustrated Story of the Trans-Canada Highway*. Vancouver: Stanton Atkins & Dosil, 2006.
Thomas Wilby, *A Motor Tour Through Canada*. London: John Lane, 1914.

Steve Turner, *Jack Kerouac: Angelheaded Hipster.* New York: Viking Penguin, 1996.

Heath Twitchell, *Northwest Epic: The Building of the Alaska Highway.* New York: St. Martin's Press, 1992.

James Mountain, *The Inhospitable Shore: An Historical Resources Study of Neys Provincial Park – Port Coldwell, Ontario.* Toronto: Ministry of Natural Resources, 1983.

Jack Kerouac, *On the Road.* New York: Viking, 1957.

Kris Lackey, *Road Frames: The American Highway Narrative.* Lincoln: University of Nebraska Press, 1997.

Maralog. Menatha, WI: Marathon, a Division of American Can Company, September–October 1960.

David L. Lewis and Laurence Goldstein, eds., *The Automobile and American Culture.* Ann Arbour: University of Michigan Press, 1980.

Deborah Paes de Barros, *Fast Cars and Bad Girls: Nomadic Subjects and Women's Road Stories.* New York: Peter Lang, 2004.

Ronald Primeau, *Romance of the Road: The Literature of the American Highway.* Bowling Green, OH: Bowling Green State University Popular Press, 1996.

CHAPTER EIGHT: VIRGIN TERRITORY

Heather Robertson and Melinda McCracken, *Magical, Mysterious Lake of the Woods.* Winnipeg, MN: Heartland Associates, 2002.

Fort Frances Times, July 2, 1936.

Marathon Mercury, September 29, 1960.

"Roads and Highways," "Trans-Canada Highway," and "Gasoline Stations." wwwcanadianecyclopedia.ca

CHAPTER NINE: CAR-NAGE

H. Laurence Ross, *Confronting Drunk Driving: Social Policy for Saving Lives.* New Haven, CT: Yale University Press, 1992.

Transportation Research Board, *Managing Speed: Review of Current Practice for Setting and Enforcing Speed Limits.* Ottawa: National Research Council, 1998.

R. Jean Wilson and Robert E. Mann, eds., *Drinking and Driving: Advances in Research and Prevention.* New York: Guilford Press, 1990.

David W. Monaghan, *Canada's "New Main Street": The Trans-Canada Highway as Idea and Reality, 1912-1956*. Ottawa: Canada Science and Technology Museum, 2002.

"Jugs of Pee." www.roadsideamerica.com/rant/pee.html.

"9/16: Terrorists Bomb Wall Street." http://crimemagazine.com/06/wallstreetbomb,0115-6.htm.

"Building Canada's Epic Ice Road." www.popularmechanics.com/outdoors/adventures/4212314. html.

"Ice Roads." www.thedieselgypsy.com/Ice%20roads-3B-Denison-2. htm.

"Battle over Roadside Shrines More Common." www.usatoday.com/news/nation/2005-07-11-roadside-memorials_x.htm.

"Road Safety: A Public Health Issue." www.who.int/features/2004/road _safety/en.

Cardiff Road Safety Centre, www.roadsafety.cardiff.gov.uk/history.

CHAPTER TEN: ROADKILL

"Study Design to Assess the Effects of Highway Median Barriers on Wildlife." Ontario Ministry of Transportation, Research and Development Branch, 1995.

"Don't Get Caught in the Rut: Driving During Fall Mating Season Can Be Deadly." www.ama.ab.ca/cps/rde/xchg/ama/web/advocacy_safety_4388.htm.

"Living With Possums." www.tvwc.org/HTML/living%20with%20possums.htm.

"U.S. Roads Kill a Million A Day." www.santacruzhub.org/pp/roadkill/stats.htm.

"Motor Vehicle Accidents Involving Turtles and Other Wildlife." www.lakejacksonturtles.org/accident.htm.

Turtle S.H.E.L.L., www.turtleshelltortue.org/educational_material/index.html.

"How Does the Rodent Cross the Road? Safely, Thanks to New Study." www.expressnews.ualberta.ca/article.cfm?id=5660.

"Collisions with Wildlife: The Rising Toll." www.who.int/features/2004/road_safety/en.

"Restrictions on Shooting from Public Roads."
   www.mrnf.gouv.qc.ca/english/publications/online/wildlife/hunting-
   regulations/general-regulations/shooting-public-road.asp.
"Caution — Animals Crossing"
   www.safety-council.org/info/traffic/roadkill.html

CHAPTER ELEVEN: READING THE ROAD
Large Canadian Roadside Attractions, ww.roadsideattractions.ca/
   alphabet.htm.
Roadside Memorials, http://roadsidememorials.com.
"Billboard [advertising]."
   http://en.wikipedia.org/wiki/Billboard_(advertising).
"Residents Split Over Roadside Memorials"
   www.rgj.com/news/stories/html/2004/03/19/66593.
   php?sp1=rgj&sp2=News&sp3=Local+News&sp5=RGJ.
   com&sp6=news&sp7=local_news
   Road Signage.
"The Inuksuk."
   www.pinnaclefarms.ca/ORIANAsite/AboutNameandLogo/Inuksuk
   New.html
Road Rules, http://roadrules.ca/?cat=68.
Brian Horeck, *Minnow Trap*. Altona, MB: Friesens, self-published, 2005.
George Straatman, *The Converging*. Timmins. ON: Amberdias Publishing,
   2006.

CHAPTER TWELVE: STREET PEOPLE
Jack Kerouac, *On the Road*. New York: Viking, 1957.
Betty Keller, *Pauline: A Biography of Pauline Johnson*. Vancouver: Douglas
   & McIntyre, 1981.
Stephen Leacock, *Sunshine Sketches of a Little Town*. London: John Lane,
   1912.
Robert Stallworthy, "What I Might Have Said," from *Things that Matter
   Now*. Calgary: Frontenac House Ltd., 2009.